THE DUFFIELD SKYLINE

AND OTHER WALKS IN DERBYSHIRE

THE DUFFIELD SKYLINE
AND OTHER WALKS IN DERBYSHIRE

LIONEL BAILEY

Illustrations by
Teresa Bailey

DB PUBLISHING

First published in Great Britain in 2010 by
The Derby Books Publishing Company Limited
3 The Parker Centre, Derby, DE21 4SZ.

ISBN 978-1-85983-774-0
Printed and bound by Cromwell Press Group, Trowbridge, Wiltshire.

CONTENTS

INTRODUCTION

For the first 24 years of my life I lived in Belper, Derbyshire, at Laund Hill, which is just over the lip of the eastern side of the Derwent Valley, just past Windy Gap. It is a continuous climb from King Street to Windy Gap, a 235ft ascent in 0.8 of a mile. When I was young my family walked a lot, and I often wonder how many times I walked or cycled up that hill.

In 1956 I joined the Belperion Cycling Club. Each weekend we would meet at the Triangle in Belper, one rider having been nominated to decide on the route and lead the run. We covered much of Derbyshire and some of Staffordshire, Leicestershire, Nottinghamshire and Yorkshire.

So the seeds were sown: a background of walking and a knowledge of the locality from the cycling club days.

Although I did some walking in the 1970s and bagged my one and only Munro, my first long walk took place in August 1982. I was asked by David Martin, a friend from schooldays then living in Winchester, to join him on a 'bit of a walk'. I eventually discovered this was the Royal Military Police & City of Chichester March, a 25-mile route designed to stretch young, trained and fit military personnel.

I completed the route and concluded that as Duffield is surrounded by hills, and other areas have walks such as the Great Gable Round, the Derwent and Howden Circuit and the Snowdon Horseshoe, then perhaps we should have something similar. So in 1983 the Duffield Skyline was created and has been held ever since as an annual event.

Dr James Mason of Duffield organised two charity walks each year. One of the walks was to raise funds for the homeless people of Derby and consisted of various routes visiting the churches covered by the Duffield Deanery. The other walk was to raise funds for the Derby Samaritans. In 2001 he died, aged 90.

On the Skyline Walk at Christmas 2001 I asked one of the regular walkers, Mike Stanier, if anyone was continuing Dr Mason's good work. Mike said that he would be organising the walks, so I offered my help. I did the route planning and the typing of the route sheets and posters, and Mike did the organisation and financial aspects. We used Dr Mason's original routes as the basis for our walks, most of which are included in this book, and it explains why so many churches appear as staging points. A church can be seen from a great distance and is a convenient and welcoming place to stop.

Other routes in the book were created to raise funds for the Friends of Babington Hospital, Belper. These are generally the shorter routes. All royalties received by me from the sale of the book will be distributed to the above charities, plus the various Mountain Rescue groups in Derbyshire.

I give special thanks to my wife Teresa for creating the illustrations and maps and to Mike Stanier for his help with the route testing.

All the routes have been walked at least twice and they are all circular. Time causes change, of course, so what I have described as a farmyard may have become a small housing estate by the time you get there.

There are two Chatsworth walks which are the same route, but one is clockwise and one anticlockwise. Having once tried to follow a route backwards on Kinder Scout, with considerable difficulty, and having been asked by the Babington Hospital group to repeat a walk because they enjoyed it so much, but in the reverse direction, I thought it worthwhile including them both.

If you are an inexperienced walker, here are a few tips.

- Check the weather forecast before leaving home.
- Walk with a companion or with a group.
- Ensure someone knows your route and timings.
- Wear strong waterproof footwear and carry warm and waterproof clothing.
- Carry water, some food, a map of the area and a mobile telephone.
- Keep to the footpath.
- Close gates.
- Keep dogs under control and on a lead if animals are in the fields.
- Walk facing oncoming traffic if there is no footpath or verge.

While every effort has been made to ensure that the information given in this book is accurate and expedient, no responsibility whatsoever can be accepted by the author for any consequences arising from the contents therein. Participation is at the walker's own risk.

Lionel Bailey
2009

Walk 1

THE DUFFIELD SKYLINE

Walk data

Distance:	10 miles
Height gain:	1,260ft
Toilets:	Pubs listed below
Refreshments:	Bluebell, Farnah Green; Strutt Arms, Milford; King William, Milford; Holly Bush, Makeney; Bridge Inn, Duffield.
Parking/Start:	St Alkmund's Church car park Duffield GR SK 349427

How to get to the start

Approaching Duffield from the south on the A6, straight on through the traffic lights at the bottom of Broadway, and take the next right turn. Approaching from the north on the A6, pass through the village centre and take the next left after Duffield Hall (currently the Derbyshire Building Society). After crossing the railway line turn right immediately. The car park is on the right.

Route summary

Duffield – Quarndon – Hazelwood – Milford – Duffield

The route is hilly and muddy in places. There is some

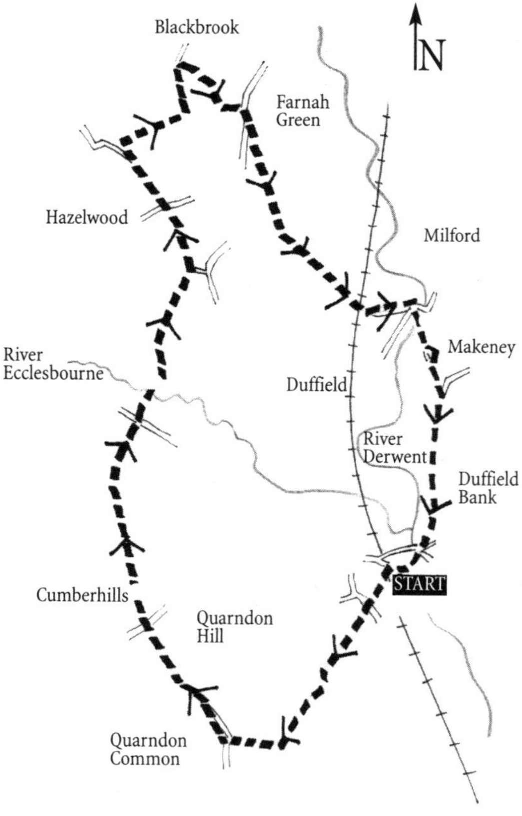

Blackbrook
N
Farnah Green
Hazelwood
Milford
Makeney
River Ecclesbourne
Duffield
River Derwent
Duffield Bank
START
Cumberhills
Quarndon Hill
Quarndon Common

road walking. At the viewpoint on Bunkers Hill there is a splendid panoramic view of Duffield and Little Eaton. The Trent valley power stations can be seen in the south. Also, the view of Belper with its red-brick mill can be seen just after entering North Lane.

ROUTE DETAILS

1 St Alkmund's Church to Cumberhill – 2.3 miles

Over metal railway bridge. Turn left immediately. Diagonally across two fields to A6. Cross A6 and take path between house Nos 40 and 38. Cross field to end of facing hedge, keeping hedge on right. Through trees and diagonally across field to top-right corner. Through stile and diagonally to left across field to top-right corner. Through stile to right and turn right uphill, keeping hedge on right. Past house and aim for vantage point known as Bunkers Hill. Follow footpath to right of houses, keeping houses on left, Burley Wood on right. Between two large trees, emerging at the end of a cul-de-sac. Turn right at end of fence of No. 16. Through holly archway to road. Turn right along The Common and after left-hand bend, at

Snowdrop Cottage, turn right through gate into fields. At end of second field, through gateway so hedge is on your left. Cross road at top of Cumberhill.

2 Cumberhill to Hazelwood Church – 2.4 miles

Down farm track past Champion Farm and ruin to Duffield/Wirksworth road. Cross Duffield/Wirksworth road. Over two stiles and walk towards bridge. Cross bridge, through gateway, keep hedge on right. Over railway line then diagonally across field. Over three stiles and then uphill with hedge on right. Through gate and farmyard on short track onto road. Turn left uphill to Hazelwood Church.

3 Hazelwood Church to Farnah Green – 2.3 miles

Carry on over crossroads, church on left. Continue towards Shottle. Turn right opposite Lane End Farm. Down single-track road to Lumb Grange and turn left onto track through new gate. Continue down track until the signpost for Midshires Way. Turn right through gateway by two large wooden posts, through stile, cross a field uphill, into wood along top of wooded valley. Over stone stile and follow footpath to road. Turn right towards Bluebell PH. After 100yds turn left onto North Lane.

4 Farnah Green to the Holly Bush PH – 2 miles

Continue south on North Lane until the A6 is reached at the Strutt Arms pub. Cross the A6 and the river bridge then turn right after the bridge. Pass the Garden Centre and turn left up Holly Bush Lane, signposted Holly Bush Inn, to the Holly Bush PH.

5 Holly Bush PH to St Alkmund's Church – 1 mile

Turn right out of the Holly Bush. Turn left onto Makeney Road. Continue and eventually cross the river bridge and back to St Alkmund's Church car park.

Walk 2

THE FOUR TOWERS CHALLENGE

Walk data

Distance:	20 miles
Height gain:	2,875ft
Toilets:	Belper Strutt Street and the Triangle, or at the pubs below.
Refreshments:	Many pubs in Belper, the Bear near Alderwasley, the Derwent Hotel at Whatstandwell, several pubs in Crich, several pubs in Heage.
Parking/Start:	Field Lane pay and display car park, Belper. GR SK 347476

How to get to the start

Field Lane is off the main A6 through Belper, between King Street and the Triangle. Approaching from the south, straight on over the Morrisons island, through the traffic lights at the bottom of King Street, pass the Lion Hotel and turn right just after the pedestrian lights.

Route summary

Belper – Milford – Alport Height – Whatstandwell – Crich – Heage – Belper

As the title suggests, this is a challenging day out. The first time we walked the route we started at 8am and finished at 5pm, with just normal stops. Belper is now included in the World Heritage Site which links Derby and Cromford. Many of the Belper mills have been demolished, but still there is the 1797 horseshoe weir that provided 22 acres of water to drive the waterwheel-powered mills. Stephenson's Sighting Tower was built to aid the construction of the railway tunnel at Milford which was completed in 1839. From Alport Height the early-morning mist can be seen rolling across the hills from Carsington Reservoir. Crich Stand is a memorial to the Sherwood Foresters and was built in 1923. From Crich Stand it is possible to see, to the south, Heage Windmill. How low down it seems to be! The windmill is the only six-sailed windmill in Britain and became operational in 1797, with four sails. It became derelict but was reopened after refurbishment in 2002.

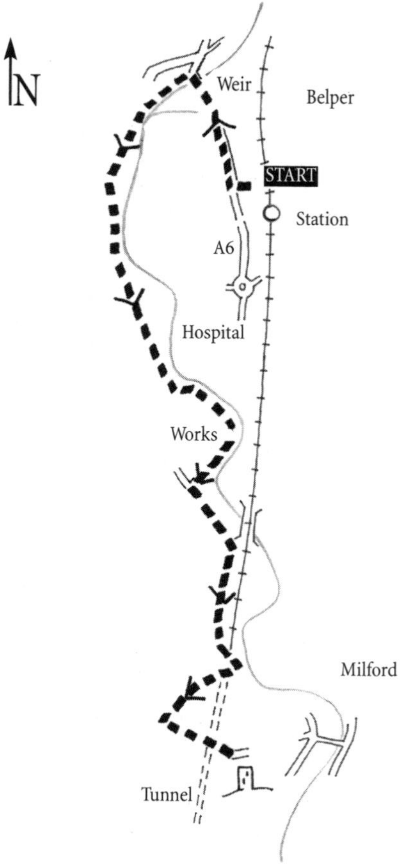
N
Weir
Belper
START
Station
A6
Hospital
Works
Milford
Tunnel

ROUTE DETAILS

1 Belper to Stephenson's Sighting Tower – 2.7 miles

Leave the car park by the north entrance. Turn left down Field Lane then right onto Bridge Street. On reaching the Triangle, keep to the left of the East Mill, under the archway, over the river bridge and turn left on a track by the side of the river. Keep on this track alongside the river, which eventually skirts the sewage works. Follow the track on a rise to Chevin Road. Turn left. After ½ mile turn right up Jackson's Lane. At the top, turn left as a small diversion is necessary to get close to Stephenson's Sighting Tower. This is the first tower.

2 Stephenson's Sighting Tower to Alport Height – 5.7 miles

After visiting the first tower, retrace your steps past the top of Jackson's Lane to the north-west, passing the shooting butts. After 1½ miles the track turns sharp left onto Farnah Green Road. Turn right and in 100 yards turn left down a drive past a bungalow. Straight on over two wooden stiles towards stone steps. Over

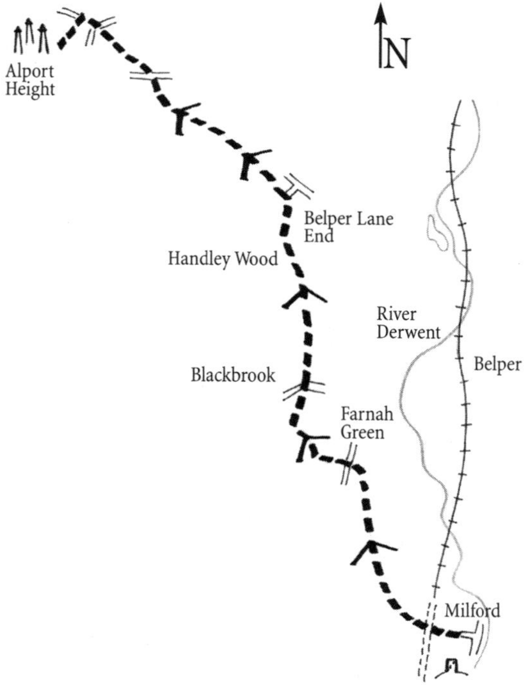

the steps and follow the path through a wood overlooking the Depths of Lumb. Into a field and follow the well-defined path onto Lumb Lane. Turn right. On reaching the road by a ford at Blackbrook turn right, pass Plains Lane then turn left up Longwalls Lane. After 1¼ miles turn left on Wilderbrook Lane for 100 yards, then turn right onto a path signed Midshires Way. After one mile the Midshires Way turns right, but continue straight on to Palerow Lane (Coneygrave Hillock). Leave Coneygrave Hillock by metal gates opposite and slightly to the left. Onto track and through gateway on the left. Aim for Alport pylons. Through stile to right of water container, through two more stiles and, keeping wall on right, aim for stile in wall ahead between two trees. Onto Peat Lane. Straight on via Back Lane then turn left through metal gate towards the radio transmitter aerials. Alport Stone is at a lower level to the south-west. This is the second tower.

3 Alport Height to Crich Stand – 4.7 miles

Leave Alport Height by entrance to lower car park then turn right onto road. Straight over crossroads into Alport Lane. On reaching Knob Lane, take footpath to right into field. Over stile, wall on right, straight ahead. Through stone stile, straight ahead,

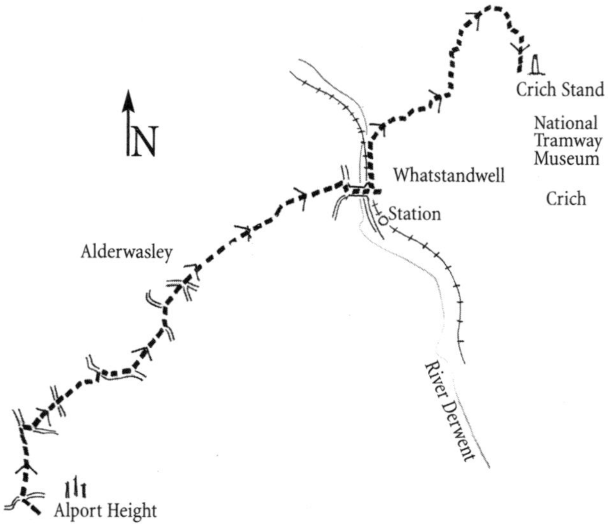

farmhouse on left, hedge on right. Through stone stile by gate. Through stile by metal gate, onto road, straight across. Over stile by metal gate, wall on left, straight ahead. Over wooden stile into small wood, across stream. Through stile, diagonally across field, through stile onto farm track. Straight across track, through stile by waymark into wood and uphill. Follow track through wood. Through stile onto road and turn right. In 200 yards at start of right-hand bend, turn left through stile 'Public Footpath'. Wall on right. After 25 yards turn right over stile so wall is on left. Continue downhill. Over stile, through two gateways, then two stiles by metal gates. Onto road by Willetts Farm.

Turn left downhill. At T-junction with Bury Hill straight ahead into Well Lane. After 15 yards turn right over stile into farmyard. Follow green sign 'Public Footpath to Whatstandwell, 1'. Over stile in wall, follow path to right towards Crich Stand. Over wooden stile, follow path straight ahead towards wood. Over stile in hedge, continue straight ahead. Stile is in top-left corner of field by wall. Through gap in hedge, straight on, wall and fence on left. At end of field, turn left over stile then turn right through gateway towards Crich Stand. Wall on right. Over stile by metal gate. Continue, hedge on right. Over stile by metal gate, hedge on right, continue downhill. Through stile to right of farm buildings. Over stile by farm drive. Keep to right of new fencing. Downhill into wood. Onto tarmac track then follow waymarked sign 'Derwent Valley Walk' and signs onto A6 road. Over river bridge. Pass Derwent Hotel. Uphill towards Crich. Turn left onto Cromford Canal towpath. After 200 yards cross the canal using metal bridge. When over bridge, take path to left. On reaching road, straight across, follow sign 'Public Footpath to Wakebridge, 1 mile'. When approaching end of wood, ignore stone stile on left, straight on over wooden stile. Over wooden stile into wood again. Over wooden stile into scrubland, Crich Stand straight ahead. On reaching road at Wakebridge, turn right then immediately left onto track signed 'Cliff Farm' and 'Public Footpath to Plaistow Green, ¾ mile'. Before reaching farmhouse turn right uphill signed 'Both paths now this way'. Through stile by metal horizontal bars. Follow sign uphill to woods 'Public Footpath to Crich, 1 mile' and 'Plaistow, ¾ mile'. On reaching tramlines, straight across, with care. Where track turns left and downhill, keep to right with square wire fence on right following lip of quarry. Follow track to Crich Stand. This is the third tower.

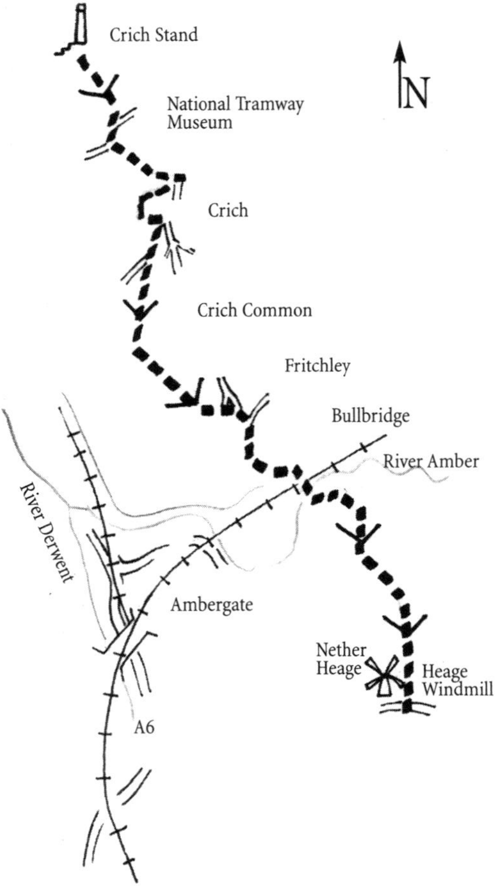
Crich Stand
N
National Tramway
Museum
Crich
Crich Common
Fritchley
Bullbridge
River Amber
River Derwent
Ambergate
Nether
Heage
Heage
Windmill
A6

4 Crich Stand to Heage Windmill – 4 miles

Follow track downhill to road. Picnics are not allowed within the boundaries of the memorial cemetery. There are toilets near the tearoom. On reaching road, turn right. On reaching the road junction turn left towards the church spire. By the front of the Jovial Dutchman pub, turn right down Jeffries Lane. On reaching Coasthill turn left downhill. On reaching a small grass circle, turn left towards the Market Place. Turn right up Sandy Lane. In 50 yards ignore signpost to Sun Lane. In another 50 yards take pathway marked 'Public Footpath'. After second stone circle through stone stile 'Public Footpath to Chadwick Nick'. Through four stiles, straight ahead. Down stone steps onto road. Turn left, downhill. At end of Chadwick Nick Lane turn left. On reaching Bull Bridge Hill, turn right downhill. Continue downhill, past Allan Lane. Past Canal Inn pub, over canal bridge. Turn left onto canal towpath signed 'Public Footpath'.

Down wooden steps, cross the railway line with care, cross the road with care and up the steps to the right of the church. Turn left onto the canal towpath.

On reaching a bridge, go under bridge and follow track round to the left to go over the bridge. Pass Waterloo Farm and follow the track uphill. At the end of the first open field follow waymark diagonally left up field towards large tree and fence. Over hidden stile. Short field, over stile. Diagonally down field and over stile. Turn right towards green dome. Over small wooden bridge. Up to hedge and through a stone stile. Turn right and keep hedge on right. Continue uphill to group of bushes. Under electricity cables and over stile. Cross access road to Heage windmill. This is the fourth Tower.

5 Heage Windmill to Belper – 2.9 miles

Follow waymarks over stile. Over stiles by equestrian training ground and on reaching road turn right down School Lane towards Nether Heage. Pass the Spanker pub then turn left down a track waymarked 'Public Footpath'. Keep to left of farm buildings. Follow waymarks. Pass Bessalone Wood. Follow clear path over several fields and access road to reservoir. Cross two more fields. Reach channel between two houses

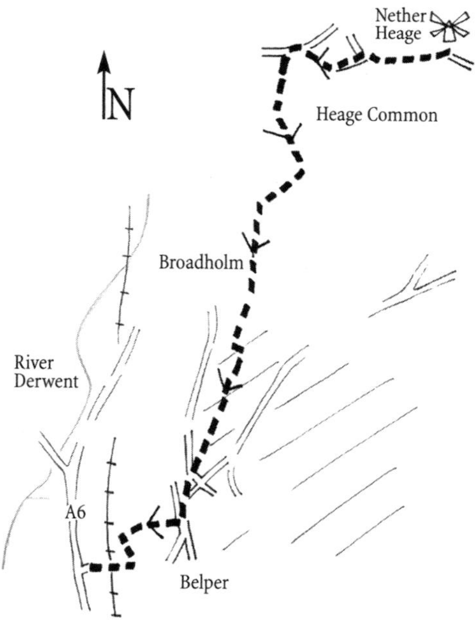

into steep road (Cherry Tree Avenue), opposite Longstone Rise. Turn left downhill and after 50 yards turn right into a channel signed 'Amber Valley DC, No cycling, No horses'. Pass a children's play area on right, across next road (Bessalone Drive) and enter channel by electricity substation. Cross Coronation Avenue into another channel which emerges at Windy Gap (the junction of Chesterfield Road, Laund Hill and Marsh Lane). Cross the road and walk downhill on Chesterfield Road, and in 200 yards, just after the Queens Head pub, turn right down a short channel, cross Swinney Lane and continue down Mill Street. At the bottom turn left onto Green Lane and shortly turn right onto Field Lane. The entrance to the car park is on the left, just over the railway bridge.

Walk 3

DUFFIELD SOUTH

Walk data

Distance:	16 miles
Height gain:	1,098ft
Toilets:	Slight diversion into Mundy Play Centre, pubs below and most churches have toilets.
Refreshments:	Bridge Inn, Duffield; Red Cow, Allestree.
Parking/Start:	St Alkmund's Church car park, Duffield. GR SK 349427

How to get to the start

Approaching Duffield from the south on the A6, straight on through the traffic lights at the bottom of Broadway, and take the next right turn. Approaching from the north on the A6, pass through the village centre and take the next left after Duffield Hall (currently the Derbyshire Building Society). After crossing the railway line turn right immediately. The car park is on the right.

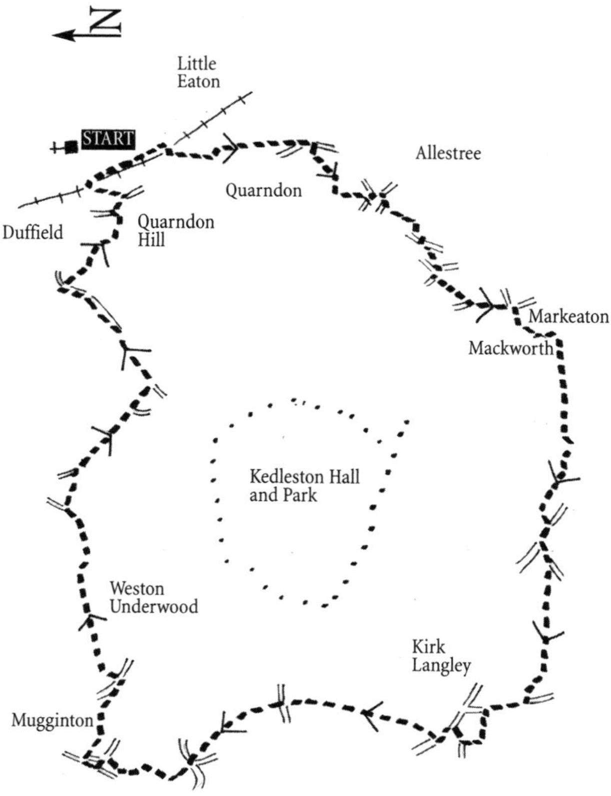
N
Little
Eaton
START
Allestree
Quarndon
Duffield
Quarndon
Hill
Markeaton
Mackworth
Kedleston Hall
and Park
Weston
Underwood
Kirk
Langley
Mugginton

Route summary

Duffield – Allestree – Mackworth – Kirk Langley – Mugginton – Duffield

The route was originally part of the Duffield Deanery walk, hence stage points are churches. The first stage is by the River Derwent and as it is necessary to walk through the centre of Allestree there is some road walking. Then it's into the country, with a little more road walking. The stage from Mugginton to Duffield is very agricultural.

ROUTE DETAILS

1 St Alkmund's Duffield to St Edmund's Allestree – 2.4 miles

Start at the monument by St Alkmund's Church. Over stile by five-bar gate. Take right fork path to corner of churchyard. Over stile into churchyard. Over stile into large field. Continue south by riverbank. Over stile, follow waymark to large gap in hedge. Through gateway with large round stone pillars. Turn right, follow waymark over stile and under bridge. Follow waymark over two stiles. Next stile by white posts in hedge. Straight across next field. Over wooden bridge and turn left on track. Over stile by bend in river. Over stile by wooden fence. Turn left over little wooden bridge and aim for stile in next field diagonally to top right-hand corner. Through right of two little gates and turn left through gateway. Stile is by right gate in hedge ahead. Onto A6 road. Turn left, cross road carefully and enter Evans Avenue. After a few yards turn right into Allestree Park. Keep to left of lake. Emerge from trees and where the information board is about birds, take the left gravel path. Cross tarmac path and turn left into trees uphill to emerge at the Evergreen Hall. Turn left and right on the road to the church.

2 St Edmund's Allestree to St Nicholas' Allestree – 1.1 miles

Leave St Edmund's, turn left then turn right opposite the Red Cow to go along Robincroft Road. Enter the small park by the black double gates. Onward uphill past the bowling green and to right of trees. Aim for top-right corner by large conifer trees and enter fenced path. At end of fences take right path with green handrail. Turn left onto road (Portreath Drive). Pass entrance to Buttermere Drive and turn right down Ness Walk. Turn left onto Birchover Way. Turn right down Clifton Road. At the end of Clifton Road turn right then left down Allestree Lane by the post box, to the church.

3 St Nicholas' Allestree to All Saints' Mackworth – 1.5 miles

Leave St Nicholas', continue down Allestree Lane. Turn left past the Markeaton pub. After new houses, turn right into Markeaton Lane, signposted Mundy Play Centre. Continue on lane for ½ mile, taking care over two bridges with no pathways and when the lane turns right past Garden Centre there is a gap in the hedge on the left and the footpath runs to the left of the hedge. When the footpath returns to the lane cross over with care to the stile on the corner and go along a clear path to Mackworth Church.

4 All Saints' Mackworth to St Michael's Kirk Langley – 2.7 miles

Leave All Saints' by drive, turn right on Lower Road

through village to Ashbourne Road, then turn right for 200 yards. Turn left onto Brun Lane, signposted to Radbourne. In 500 yards on a bend with black, white and red posts, just after power lines, turn right over stile in new fence. Keep to left-hand side of field, parallel with power lines. Stile is in top-left corner by tree house. Over stile into field, straight ahead. Next stile is halfway along facing hedge to left of two large trees. Through what appears to be someone's garden. Stile is in top-right corner behind large conifer trees. Turn left up lane. At junction cross to footpath between hedges to left of 'The Bungalow'. Over stile into field, keep hedge on left. After next stile turn left on drive. Turn right down Moor Lane. Continue to the 30mph sign where there is a footpath signed on the left. Cross two fields then go through a stile to left of large tree into a playing field and on to Kirk Langley Church.

5 St Michael's Kirk Langley to All Saints' Mugginton – 2.9 miles

Leave St Michael's and turn right to Ashbourne Road. Turn left and in about 60 yards past the Kirk Langley entry sign find a waymarked stile in the hedge on the right. The next stile is in the corner of the field, waymarked, go to right of a shed and take slippery bridge into field. Keep along left edge of field to stile in hedge on brow of hill. Cross field to next stile onto Flagshaw Lane. Take stile opposite taking left of the two waymarked paths to stile in hedge on left, by most dominant post. Continue diagonally across field to corner and through an iron gate. Onward to stile in fence ahead and aim across field for left of fourth tree from right, due north. Cross stile and keep round left edge of field. Cross into field by water trough, go between Buck Hazels Farm and brick shelter to cross lane via stile. Through stile immediately opposite. Cross field to stile just round left corner of field facing. Follow left field boundary. Follow waymark into small wood, over stile into field. Over stile. Cross field to open gate. Over field to large oak tree. Through gateway, turn left keeping hedge on left towards waymarked stile. Cross fence, down field to bottom left corner by large oak tree. Cross the lane to stile opposite and onward to bridge and continue to plank and rail bridge to cross culvert. Diagonally to the right, over stile and follow direction arrows with fence on right. Over stile, turn right. Immediately turn left then right in 100 yards towards bridge and cross stream. Over stile into copse and out into field. Straight up field, stile is at top-left corner. Go left into Mugginton.

6 All Saints' Mugginton to St Alkmund's Duffield – 5.1 miles

Leave Mugginton Church and turn left up hill, turn right opposite school through farmyard. Down track. At end of lane carry straight on, towards village of Weston Underwood. Stile is at bottom left-hand corner of field by holly hedge. Cross over stream on bridge. Stile is in top right-hand corner of next field. Go to main road then turn right. After 200 yards turn left down Burland Green Lane. Turn right on indicated public footpath after derestricted signs. Over gate into open field. Aim to right of wood (Draycott Plantation). Over stile and small bridge over stream. Path is in lower area in marshy ground, to right of large tree. Then cross over small stream and cross two open fields. Through small waymarked gate. Cross open field towards tree, over waymarked stile, keep hedge on left, over stile which is halfway down field, at end of continuous hedge. Down middle of large field. Aim for tree 100 yards to right of bottom left-hand corner. Cross bridge and aim for top left-hand corner of field. Through gate and onto green track. After 200 yards, as track turns left, through stile and keep hedge on left. Aim for road (Woodfall Lane), stile is in top left-hand corner, one field away from farm buildings. Turn right towards Quarndon. At right bend in road go straight ahead. Cross field diagonally round tree, hedge on right. Onto road and turn left. Down Cumberhills Road, turn right down Broadway. On reaching the A6 road, cross at the traffic lights and turn right. After 100 yards turn left into a field and follow the path to the corner. Over the stile and turn right to cross the metal bridge over the railway line back to St Alkmund's.

Walk 4

DUFFIELD NORTH

Walk data

Distance:	15 miles
Height gain:	1,993ft
Toilets:	Strutt Street, Belper. Pubs as below and most churches have toilets.
Refreshments:	Pubs in Duffield, Holbrook, Milford, Belper and Ambergate.
Parking/Start:	St Alkmund's Church car park, Duffield. GR SK 349427

How to get to the start

Approaching Duffield from the south on the A6, straight on through the traffic lights at the bottom of Broadway, and take the next right turn. Approaching from the north on the A6, pass through the village centre and take the next left after Duffield Hall (currently the Derbyshire Building Society). After crossing the railway line turn right immediately. The car park is on the right.

Route summary

Duffield – Holbrook – Milford – Belper – Ambergate – Belper – Duffield

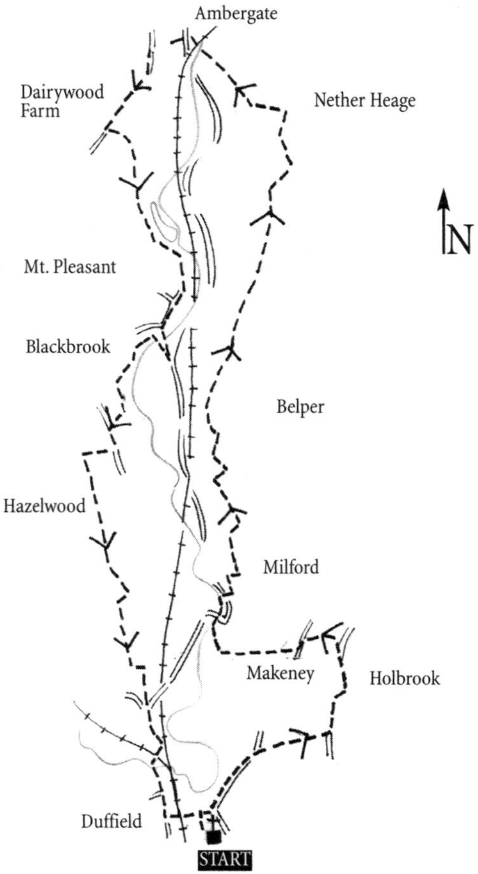
Ambergate
Dairywood Farm
Nether Heage
N
Mt. Pleasant
Blackbrook
Belper
Hazelwood
Milford
Makeney
Holbrook
Duffield
START

A walk following the Derwent Valley, mainly in fields but with some road walking in Belper. The remaining industrial heritage of Milford and Belper is seen on this walk.

ROUTE DETAILS

1 St Alkmund's Duffield to St Michael's Holbrook – 1.7 miles

Leave St Alkmund's, over stile towards river, over river bridge, turn left towards Makeney, after 200 yards turn right on track to Manor Quarry signposted 'Holbrook, 2', into wood to right of Rose Cottage sign, along path with hedges either side, over stile into wood, follow track with posts and squared netting on your left. Out of wood, hedge on right, stile is in top right-hand corner of field. Head to right of house with conservatory. Through stile onto road. Past two houses, after 200 yards turn left through stile, across corner of field, through a wood and over small bridge, into open field. Diagonally across field onto the road. Turn left up the hill to the church.

2 St Michael's Holbrook to Holy Trinity Milford – 1.3 miles

Leave St Michael's, turn left up the hill, take the left-hand road, turn left up Mellors Lane. At the T-junction turn left then in about 50 yards turn right onto a path signposted 'Milford, 1'. Follow the path downhill. On approaching houses at bottom of slope keep hedge on left. Down steps bringing you out at the Holly Bush PH. Turn right downhill and turn right again opposite the Makeney Hall Hotel. Pass the Garden Centre to join the A6 and keep right to Milford Church.

3 Holy Trinity Milford to St Swithun's Belper – 1.1 miles

Leave Holy Trinity, go up the 'Church Steps', turn left along Hopping Hill Terrace West, on reaching road turn right up hill. Continue past entrance to 'Bridge View'. As road enters a wood, find steps on your left and waymarked path with wood on your right. At next wood follow path to right of wood – BEWARE LOW BRANCHES. Turn left onto farm track. Continue along track to Holbrook Road, turn left for 50 yards to church.

4 St Swithun's Belper to St Peter's Belper – 0.9 miles

Leave St Swithun's to go up Holbrook Road and where the road turns right, take footpath to the left to walk along the level path. When the path begins to drop by iron railings continue by railings and straight on through edge of wood, aiming for St Peter's Tower, coming out on edge of playing field. About 100 yards before the houses leave the playing field by a gap on your right and continue keeping hedge on your left. Keep straight on to come out onto New Breck Road. Continue up Queen Street and Market Place to St Peter's.

5 St Peter's Belper to St Anne's Ambergate – 2.9 miles

Leave St Peter's Churchyard by the East Gate, turn left up Chesterfield Road. In about 600 yards fork left up Crich Lane and just after Marsh Lane turn right onto footpath signposted 'AVBC, No Cycling, No Horses' by corner of stone house. Continue on this path crossing two roads and at the third, Longstone Drive, turn left and find an unsigned path between houses 60 and 62.

This brings you into open country with a well-marked path. The sixth field has a wood on the right. Pass the wood and by the first gate keep on the farm track on the right with the hedge on your right. Carry on this track past a farmhouse and factory. On reaching the road turn left up the hill, carry on straight across the crossroads at the top of the hill and down Newbridge Road to the A6. Cross the A6 to St Anne's.

6 St Anne's Ambergate to Christ Church Belper – 2.6 miles

Leave St Anne's and turn left onto Holly Lane to cross the river. Bear left up the hill then turn left onto Whitewells Lane signposted Blackbrook. In about three quarters of a mile you come to a wood on your left. Immediately past the wood there is a stone stile on the left, opposite a farm entrance. Go over the stile, down steps and follow the wall on the left to the next stile. Across a field to bottom of the wood on your right, follow wall on your right to gate/stile. Continue straight ahead on farm track to next gate/stile, then turn right onto lane past target area of old firing range.

Continue on lane which becomes Wyver Lane and comes out onto Bridge Foot. Turn left to cross the river to Christ Church.

7 Christ Church Belper to St Alkmund's Duffield – 4.3 miles

Leave Christ Church and return over river. Immediately turn left onto waymarked lane which shortly becomes a field path. After two fields cross brook and drive, follow waymark, keep wall on your right. At the second gate in hedge go through a waymarked stile, follow path through wall and gap in hedge. Follow stone-paved path to top of bank and aim for left-hand end of garden wall skirting property. Go over wooden stile into driveway to come out into Chevin Road. Turn left and in 150 yards turn right onto signed footpath. Follow steep path with wall on your right for two fields and through stile onto ancient North Lane. Turn left and follow track for one mile. As track starts to descend turn right by large flat green field and Midshires Way sign. Down steep path to stile, diagonally left across field, down track to right of golf course, over stream, over two stiles to road. Turn right, past clubhouse and onto A6. Straight ahead on A6 through Duffield village. Turn left after the Derbyshire Building Society HQ and after crossing the railway bridge turn right back to St Alkmund's.

Walk 5

DUFFIELD WEST

Walk data

Distance:	14 miles
Height gain:	1,614ft
Toilets:	See pubs below.
Refreshments:	Pubs in Duffield and Turnditch.
Parking/Start:	St Alkmund's Church car park, Duffield. GR SK 349427

How to get to the start

Approaching Duffield from the south on the A6, straight on through the traffic lights at the bottom of Broadway, and take the next right turn. Approaching from the north on the A6, pass through the village centre and take the next left after Duffield Hall (currently the Derbyshire Building Society). After crossing the railway line turn right immediately. The car park is on the right.

Route summary

Duffield – Hazelwood – Turnditch – Mugginton – Quarndon – Duffield

This route is mainly through fields, which, depending

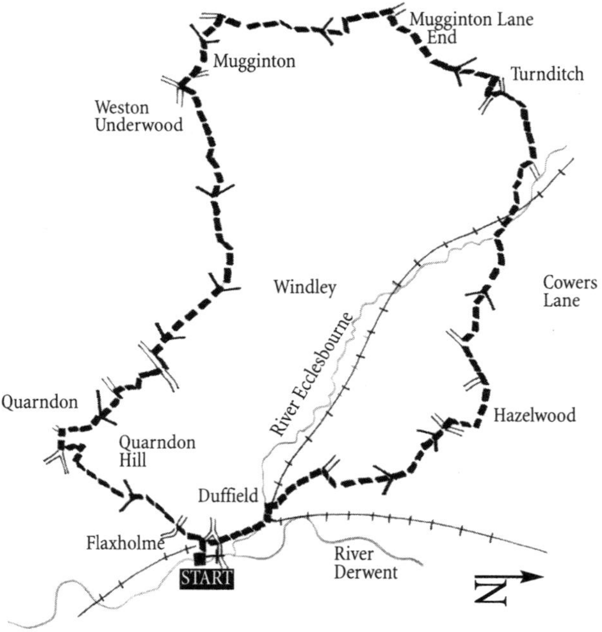

on the time of year, are set with crops. There is some road walking. At the viewpoint on Bunkers Hill there is a splendid panoramic view of Duffield and Little Eaton. The Trent Valley power stations can be seen in the south.

ROUTE DETAILS

1 St Alkmund's Duffield to St John's Hazelwood – 2.8 miles

Leave St Alkmund's and walk along Donald Hawley Way, approximately north. Turn left under the railway line and then right alongside the Ecclesbourne River. Turn left onto Chapel Street then right through a small path to reach the A6 by the King's Head. Cross the road using the pedestrian crossing and turn right. At the HSBC bank keep left up King Street. On reaching the cemetery, turn right down Chevin Road then left onto a footpath by 'Do not exceed 20' sign. In 150 yards turn right by metal gate. Over three stiles, straight ahead, hedge on right. Turn left on reaching hedge bordering golf course. Over small stream. Uphill diagonally across a field towards a stile in the wall ahead. Over stile and turn left towards Hazelwood Hall Farm. Onto Spring Hollow and turn right uphill. After Rose Cottage turn left onto footpath by stone wall. Through small gate, over two stiles, hedge on left. Follow yellow waymark to hedge on horizon. Onto Goodwins Lane and turn left towards St John's.

2 St John's Hazelwood to All Saints' Turnditch – 2.3 miles

Leave St John's and turn right down Hob Hill. Just past 'Kalamundra', turn right over stile on farm track, take stile on left about 10 yards past a gate. Path goes down right side of field next to a wood, stile is in corner. Follow hedge to next stile then left along hedge and right at corner. In 100 yards through gate on left and down farm track on left of hedge. When track becomes cement go on and take stile straight ahead, to left of metal gate and skirt around to right of farm boundary to come onto Wirksworth Road. Cross the road and take stile about 20 yards up road. Cross field diagonally to find stile onto level crossing. Cross railway, turn right between ditch and railway, on coming to stile in 30 yards turn left, pass left of wooden hut to cross Ecclesbourne River. Bear right to corner of abutting field then to right of sewage works and find stile in corner onto lane. Lane takes you to Ashbourne Road. Turn left up hill to All Saints'.

3 All Saints' Turnditch to All Saints' Mugginton – 2.8 miles

Leave Turnditch Church to go up the hill. Opposite the Tiger PH turn left along Windley Lane. In about 100 yards at end of wood on right turn right down farm lane which turns left in about 150 yards. Continue on this track for about 400 yards to go through a metal gate straight ahead. Continue with hedge on left for two fields to find footbridge over stream. Bear right diagonally across field to corner where there are two gates. Take the right-hand one and follow hedge on left. On going through gate into next field follow cart track to gate on right of farm, through this and straight ahead to waymarked gate and skirt to right of farm property to find stile into lane.

Turn right up lane and onto road. Turn left and follow road for half a mile. After left-hand bend turn right onto footpath. Stile is in thick undergrowth. Keep hedge on right, through stile, wood (Old Covert) on right. Across house drive down to waymarked stile and across next field, wood on right. At end of wood, through a group of trees and over waymarked stile.

Straight ahead through open field. Stile is 100 yards from bottom right corner of field, by tree. Across next field to stile and into what seems to be a lawned garden. Aim for top-left corner, stile is by white gate, beyond a circular stone well. Onto road, turn right down road to All Saints'.

4 All Saints' Mugginton to St Paul's Quarndon – 4.2 miles

Leave Mugginton Church and turn left up hill, turn right opposite school through new houses. Down track. At end of lane carry straight on, towards village of Weston Underwood. Stile is at bottom-left corner of field by holly hedge. Cross over stream on bridge. Stile is in top-right corner of next field. Go to main road then turn right. After 200 yards turn left down Burland Green Lane. Turn right on indicated public footpath after derestricted signs. Over gate into open field. Aim to right of wood (Draycott Plantation). Over stile and small bridge over stream. Path is in lower area in marshy ground, to right of large tree. Then cross over small stream and across two open fields. Through small waymarked gate. Cross open field towards tree, over waymarked stile, keep hedge on left, over stile which is halfway down field, at end of continuous hedge. Down middle of large field. If rough ploughing makes progress impossible, walk round the field to the left. Aim for tree 100 yards to right of bottom-left corner. Cross bridge and aim for top-left corner of field. Again use the left side if progress impossible. Through gate and onto green track. After 200 yards, as track turns left, through stile and keep hedge on left. Aim for road (Woodfall Lane), stile is in top-left corner, one field away from farm buildings. Turn right towards Quarndon. At right bend in road go straight ahead. Cross field diagonally round tree, hedge on right. Onto road and turn left. After 100 yards turn right through stile into field opposite a white house signed 'Public Footpath to Quarndon, 2', with hedge on right. Over stile so hedge is on left. Through stile then through metal gate onto road. Turn left and follow road to St Paul's.

5 St Paul's Quarndon to St Alkmund's Duffield – 1.7 miles

Leave Quarndon Church, turn right and right again down Burley Lane. Turn left up Montpelier. Take footpath on right between 'Treetops' and No. 8. At T-junction turn right along grassy path and then on right side of Burley Wood. On coming out into field the path goes along by the hedge, but, except in the dark, walkers should bear right and go to the three oak trees that mark the top of Bunkers Hill (to see the view). Descend to Burley Wood farm to rejoin the path and go through stile about 100 yards past the house. Keep right along edge of field and ongoing through broken hedge, diagonally across field to waymarked stile about 100 yards to right of large oak tree. From there the path goes straight towards Duffield Church. On reaching the A6 (heavy traffic) cross to stile immediately opposite and cross two fields to footbridge over railway line to St Alkmund's.

Walk 6

DUFFIELD EAST – 1

Walk data

Distance:	10 miles
Height gain:	1,027ft
Toilets:	Pub below. Most churches have toilets.
Refreshments:	Bell and Harp pub, Little Eaton.
Parking/Start:	St Alkmund's Church car park, Duffield. GR SK 349427

How to get to the start

Approaching Duffield from the south on the A6, straight on through the traffic lights at the bottom of Broadway, and take the next right turn. Approaching from the north on the A6, pass through the village centre and take the next left after Duffield Hall (currently the Derbyshire Building Society). After crossing the railway line turn right immediately. The car park is on the right.

Route summary

Duffield – Breadsall – Morley – Little Eaton – Duffield

This route passes the base of the chimney of Peckwash

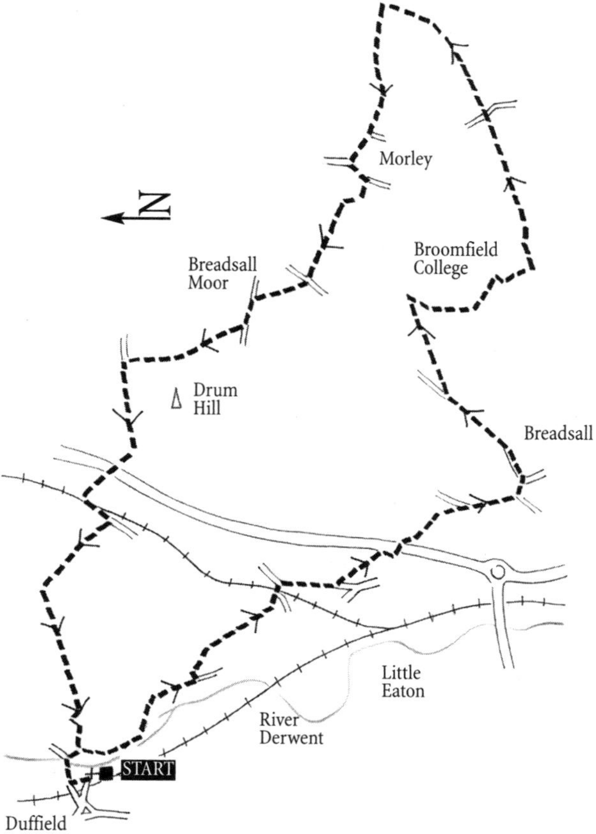
N
Morley
Breadsall Moor
Broomfield College
Drum Hill
Breadsall
Little Eaton
River Derwent
START
Duffield

Mill, originally a corn mill in the 13th century then a paper mill in the mid-19th century. The chimney was built in 1895. After the Bell and Harp the distance back to Duffield is short, but a very steep climb.

ROUTE DETAILS

1 Duffield to Breadsall – 2.8 miles

Leave church car park by stile opposite War Memorial and walk diagonally across field to riverside path. Cross river bridge, turn right past Bridge Inn and turn right down a narrow public footpath by telegraph post 24 and signposted 'Footpath to Eaton Bank'. Straight on over two stiles and over stile into wood. Follow path past base of Peckwash Mill chimney, up fenced path onto road. Turn right. Follow Eaton Bank for 300 yards and just past the last house turn left by waymark post 'Public Footpath'. Walk uphill on an old cobbled path. In a few yards take first turning after cobbles finish to walk up through the woods, passing an old quarry on the left. At the top of the hill turn right to follow a wider path, through a narrow stile and follow a wall on the left to the field corner. Cross the stile and keep right to follow a minor road. In 300 yards bear left by the house sign 'Sea Wife', pass three houses on the left and follow a narrow minor road behind the church. In 150 yards bear right down a flight of steps to join a minor road. In a few yards, on reaching the village road in Little Eaton, keep straight on along 'The Town', over the railway level crossing then cross the Alfreton Road using the pedestrian crossing. Turn right to follow the road for 400 yards. Just past New Inn Lane on the right, turn left signed 'Public Footpath To Breadsall' by a brown fence. Cross two stiles. Bear right to pass behind a builder's yard. Follow a fence on the right and in the field corner cross a stile. Walk straight ahead up a fenced path. On reaching the underpass below the A38 take the right-hand track. Follow the undulating path to a gate and pass through. Keep straight on with a hedge on your left heading for the spire of Breadsall Church. On reaching a wide gap in the hedge turn left and in a few yards turn to the right so hedge is on your right. Pass through a gate and walk down Rectory Lane. At the end of Rectory Lane turn left towards the church.

2 Breadsall to Morley – 3.6 miles

Leave Breadsall Church uphill on Moor Road towards Breadsall Priory. The road soon becomes derestricted, so walk on the grass verge on the left-hand side of the road. After half a mile turn right by brown metal gates onto footpath signed 'Footpath'. Path is diagonally across first field. In second field keep hedge on your left. At end of second field a track is reached. Cross track into hedge and take right of two stiles. Keep hedge on right. At end of field stile is in top right-hand corner, signed 'Circular Walk 12'. Through stile and gate onto golf course. Straight ahead, keep to left of small copse, follow waymarked post to stile in top left corner, avoiding golf greens. Over stile and into wood. Out of wood along edge of field, hedge on left. Over stile onto track. Over track and over stile into field towards wood and road. Over two stiles which are to right of large trees. Across field towards notice board. Over stile onto road.

Turn left uphill. After 150 yards cross road and turn right onto path signposted 'Public Footpath' and 'Footpath 19'. Keep fence on left. Stile is in top-left corner. Over three stiles, keep hedge/wood/fence on right. Over stile onto track, over track and over stile into field towards stile straight ahead. Across field , over stile into field, hedge on right. Over stile and over new bridge. Round edge of field, keep hedge on right. At end of hedge straight on across field. Over stile onto road. Beware traffic coming around bend from right. Cross road, over cattle grid onto track. Where farm track swings sharp left, carry straight on with trees and fence on the right. Through metal gate into large field, hedge on left. Over stile at end of field, immediately over new stile, straight ahead with hedge on right. Over stile marked with yellow arrow on green circle. Turn left towards metal gate. Over stile. Turn left through gate onto Midshires Way/Centenary Way/Walk 3. Follow track and road towards Morley Church. Turn right onto Church Lane. Turn right into church grounds signposted 'Public Footpath to Church'.

3 Morley to Little Eaton – 2.6 miles

Leave Morley Church uphill and at T-junction at top of hill turn left and cross road. Do not take the path opposite Church Road. Continue along the road for 150 yards and turn right up a tarmac drive. Over stile and follow Centenary Way sign. Over stile by metal gate and immediately turn right over stile signed Centenary Way and over bridge. Turn left onto track. Where track turns left at end of trees, walk straight ahead across field. Over stile onto road. Turn right. Come out of Morley Almshouses Lane onto Moor Road. Directly across to follow Centenary Way. Follow path through grassy field into wood then trees on your left. Come out onto Morley Lane, opposite Priory Cottages. Turn left downhill. After 100 yards turn right signed Public Footpath and Centenary Way. Across two fields with waymarked stiles. Onto golf course, turn left towards wall and walk on grass track with wall on your left. Follow track into trees. Downhill through trees and on reaching a wide, well-defined track, turn left. After half a mile turn right into wood on well-defined track towards wooden gate. Onto path towards A38. Through gate towards underpass. Under A38 and follow track round to left. Cross road and over railway line. On reaching road turn left reaching the Bell and Harp shortly.

4 Little Eaton to Duffield – 1.3 miles

Past the Bell and Harp, turn right up Whittaker Lane. The lane becomes a path through trees. Continue straight on path. Over stile into field, hedge on left. Straight on through gate, oak trees on right. Straight on through gate, follow Centenary Way sign hedge on left. Straight on through gate. Through stile on left, keep hedge on right. Stile is in top-right corner. Into wood, straight ahead, out of wood, through overgrown field. Downhill and down steps, turn left onto road by white double garage. Turn right by electricity substation, downhill to the Bridge pub, over the river bridge and back to the car park.

Walk 7

DUFFIELD EAST – 2

Walk data

Distance:	8 miles
Height gain:	966ft
Toilets:	Pubs below. Most churches have toilets.
Refreshments:	Coach and Horses pub, Horsley; Bell and Harp pub, Little Eaton.
Parking/Start:	St Alkmund's Church car park, Duffield. GR SK 349427

How to get to the start

Approaching Duffield from the south on the A6, straight on through the traffic lights at the bottom of Broadway, and take the next right turn. Approaching from the north on the A6, pass through the village centre and take the next left after Duffield Hall (currently the Derbyshire Building Society). After crossing the railway line turn right immediately. The car park is on the right.

Route summary

Duffield – Horsley – Brackley Gate – Little Eaton – Duffield

An interesting, but not unique, feature of this walk is a footpath that appears to cross someone's back garden. The route also crosses Ryknield Street.

ROUTE DETAILS

1 St Alkmund's Church Duffield to Horsley Church – 2.5 miles

Start from the War Memorial at St Alkmund's Church. Over the stile towards the river. Next stile is in top-left corner of the field. Over stile and towards road, turn right and over river bridge. Turn left uphill signposted 'Makeney, Holbrook'. After 300 yards turn right onto track with sign 'Manor Quarry' and signposted 'Public Footpath, Holbrook, 2'. Keep to right of sign 'Rose Cottage' on uphill woodland track, up stony steep path with steps, follow path between fields and wood. Through stile, path is to the right.

Over fence into wood. Follow main right track with squared netting on fence on left. Over small stream. Emerge from wood, straight ahead, hedge on right. Through archway in hedge, straight ahead. On reaching buildings, turn left over stile onto

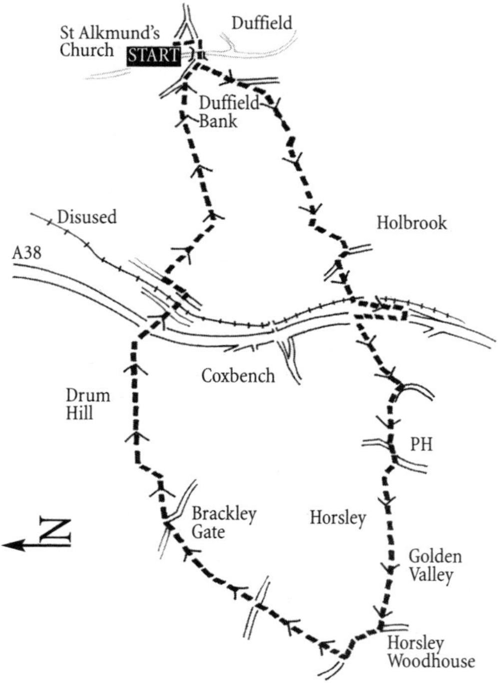

track. In 75 yards turn right by double gates downhill across field.

Twenty-five yards from bottom-left corner through stile into what appears to be a back garden.

Path is to left of block built building. Emerge onto road and turn right.

In 10 yards turn left over stile into field signed 'Public Footpath'. Straight ahead across field. Over small bridge and railway line. Over stile onto Derby/Ripley road. Cross road and turn left towards A38 interchange. Over slip road and under A38 bridge. Turn right up A38 slip road signposted 'Derby' and in a few yards turn left onto track signposted 'Public Footpath'. Over stile, follow yellow arrow, hedge on right. Continue and over stile. Continue ahead. Over stile in high hedge and immediately turn left uphill, hedge on left. Over stile, keep to path straight ahead, hedge on left. At bottom of hill bear right then turn left uphill to right of electricity pylon. Through stile by church, through stile by church entrance and turn right.

2 Horsley Church to Brackley Gate – 2.5 miles

Carry on through village, past road junction, past Coach and Horses pub. 75 yards after the pub turn right by house No. 8, signposted 'Public Footpath,

Horsley Woodhouse, Smalley Mill'. Through stile by metal gate, straight ahead to gate in hedge. Through new galvanized metal kissing gate. Turn right towards second kissing gate. Do not go through the second gate but turn left with hedge and golf course on right. Continue through third kissing gate. Through stone stile, continue ahead, hedge on right. Through fourth kissing gate, continue ahead, to stile in hedge. Diagonally across field to bridge by large trees in bottom right corner. Over railway sleeper bridge uphill to top-right corner. Through gateway, hedge on right.

Turn right over stile which is 50 yards before the end of the field. Continue on fenced path, over small planked bridge and stile, follow diagonal path to right. Over stile into field, straight ahead, follow path through hedge, hedge on right. Over stile onto road. Cross road onto footpath and turn right uphill. After 200 yards turn right over stile by wooden gate opposite house No. 38.

Over wooden stile, hedge on left. Before reaching facing hedge with metal gate, branch right, through gap in hedge and over small bridge. Follow path downhill, hedge on left. Over stile, continue ahead, hedge on left. Next stile is by small bridge near electricity line pole. Over stile by metal gates onto road. Straight across road, over stile into field signposted 'Public Footpath Cloves Hill'. Uphill, hedge on right. Over stile in hedge, straight ahead. Through stile by cast-iron inverted dome. Note change from hedges to walls. Straight ahead, wall on right. Through two stiles, wall on right then over stone step stile onto road. Turn right.

3 Brackley Gate to the Bell and Harp, Little Eaton – 1.3 miles

As road swings to the right in 50 yards carry straight on indicated as 'No Through Road'. Ahead into wood on track for 1 mile. Within sight and sound of the A38 turn right onto track by three large rocks signposted 'Public Bridleway'.

Follow 'Midshires Way' waymarker, through gate and under the A38. Follow path to Derby/Ripley road. Straight across road, follow 'Midshires Way' waymarker. Cross railway line, through metal gate onto road. Turn left to the Bell and Harp pub.

4 Bell and Harp Little Eaton to St Alkmund's Church, Duffield – 1.5 miles

Continue from the Bell and Harp and in a few yards turn right onto Whittaker Lane, signposted 'Public Bridleway'. Continue uphill and the road becomes a track. Track enters wood and near top of hill ignore stile and signs to left. Continue ahead. Over wooden stile into field. Through three wooden gates, hedge on left. 10 yards after third wooden gate over stile so that hedge is on right. Enter wood by stile at top-right of field. Follow 'Centenary Way' signs. Path is left, downhill. Down steps. On reaching gable end of house, turn left, signposted 'Public Footpath'. On reaching road, turn right downhill to the Bridge Inn. Turn left over river bridge and proceed back to the church car park.

Walk 8

DUFFIELD EAST – 3

Walk data

Distance:	5½ miles
Height gain:	577ft
Toilets:	Pubs below.
Refreshments:	Three pubs in Holbrook; Holly Bush, Makeney; Bridge Inn, Duffield.
Parking/Start:	St Alkmund's Church car park, Duffield. GR SK 349427

How to get to the start

Approaching Duffield from the south on the A6, straight on through the traffic lights at the bottom of Broadway, and take the next right turn. Approaching from the north on the A6, pass through the village centre and take the next left after Duffield Hall (currently the Derbyshire Building Society). After crossing the railway line turn right immediately. The car park is on the right.

Route summary

Duffield – Holbrook – Duffield

A pleasant short walk. This route passes the base of the

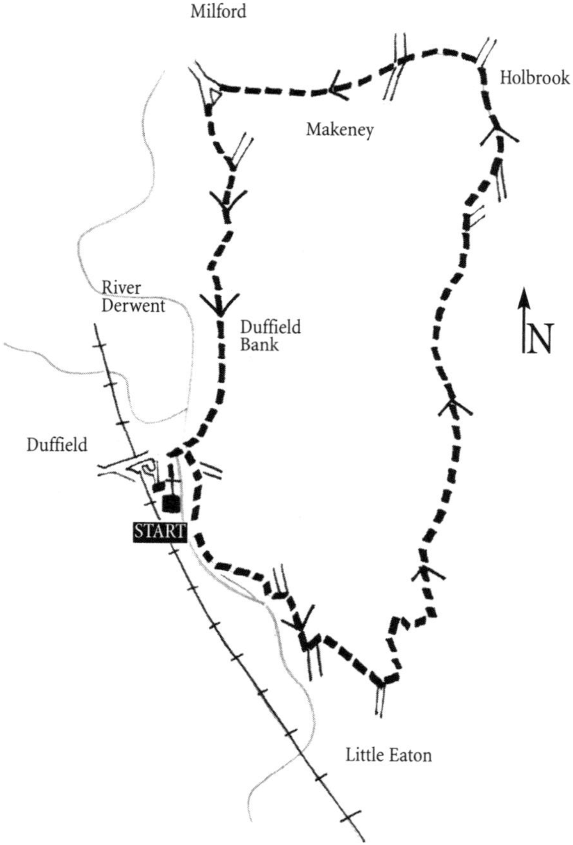
Milford
Holbrook
Makeney
River Derwent
Duffield Bank
N
Duffield
START
Little Eaton

chimney of Peckwash Mill, originally a corn mill in the 13th century that became a paper mill in the mid-19th century. The chimney was built in 1895. For a short distance the route follows the ancient Portway, a trackway from Nottingham to Castleton.

ROUTE DETAILS

1 St Alkmund's Church to Holbrook – 3 miles

Walk towards War Memorial Cross outside church gate. Turn sharp left and enter field over low stile marked 'Midshires Way'. Cross field diagonally to top-left corner. Over stile and follow path to left along river bank. Cross bridge and turn right past the Bridge Inn. Turn sharp right by telephone post 24 down narrow path. Straight on over two stiles and continue to small stile marked 'Circular Walk 9'. Follow path through wood past base of Peckwash Mill chimney, up slope and onto main road. Turn right and follow road for 300 yards, cross road and turn sharp left up track, signed 'Circular Walk 9'. After a few yards, turn right up a steep narrow path past base of large tree. Follow path up through wood and up a short steep slope onto a main track. Turn right, through squeeze gap between wall and gate, follow path to stile. Over stile, turn left (Circular Walk 9). Up hill on metalled lane, which becomes a track, to Park Farm House. Cross yard to stile (Circular Walk 9). Over stile and follow path down right side of field. At bottom of field turn left, signposted to Holbrook. Follow path through fields, still following 'Circular Walk 9'. Over stile in small hollow, up slope and over stile. Keep to right of field, follow track round corner and pass through gap 'Circular Walk 9'. Diagonally across field, over stile and continue diagonally. Follow track round a holly tree and diagonally left to next stile. There are three signs on the stile. 'Circular Walk 9', 'Midshires Way' and 'Derwent Valley Walk'. Ignore the first two and follow 'Derwent Valley Walk' sign. Straight on and over next stile, 'Public Footpath' sign. Diagonally left and squeeze through gap. Follow path along field edge and over stile (Derwent Valley Walk). Through gap with farm on right. Continue following 'Derwent Valley Walk' signs, diagonally across field towards stone house. Through stile, past the front of two houses and follow road downhill. After a short distance, through gap in stone wall on left (Derwent Valley Walk), across corner of field into wood. Through stile and across bridge, through stile, follow path diagonally to right down field to road. Through gap in wall onto road (Port Way). Turn left uphill to Holbrook.

2 Holbrook to St Alkmund's Church – 2½ miles

Enter Church Street then turn left up Mellor's Lane. At the T-junction turn left and in 10 yards turn right onto a footpath 'Milford, 1'. Through stile, downhill, over stile, follow path on left of field. Through stile, across small field, hedge on left. Over stile, down steps onto road opposite the Holly Bush PH. Turn left down Holly Bush Lane then left onto Makeney Road. Continue to the river bridge, over the river and back to the car park.

Walk 9

DUFFIELD EAST – 4

Walk data

Distance:	15 miles
Height gain:	1,668ft
Toilets:	Duffield Chapel Street, also pubs below.
Refreshments:	Pubs in Milford, Makeney, Holbrook, Little Eaton and Duffield.
Parking/Start:	St Alkmund's Church car park, Duffield. GR SK 349427

How to get to the start

Approaching Duffield from the south on the A6, straight on through the traffic lights at the bottom of Broadway, and take the next right turn. Approaching from the north on the A6, pass through the village centre and take the next left after Duffield Hall (currently the Derbyshire Building Society). After crossing the railway line turn right immediately. The car park is on the right.

Route summary

Duffield – Hazelwood – Milford – Holbrook – Breadsall – Little Eaton – Duffield

Mainly fields with quite a bit of road walking. It is necessary to navigate an interchange of the A38. On the last stage you will encounter the narrowest stile, ever.

ROUTE DETAILS

1 St Alkmund's Duffield to St John's Hazelwood – 2.9 miles

Leave the church car park on Donald Hawley Way, approximately north. Turn left under the railway line and then right alongside the river.

Turn left onto Chapel Street then right through a small path to reach the A6 by the King's Head. Cross the road using the pedestrian crossing and turn right. At the HSBC bank keep left up King Street. On reaching the cemetery, turn right down Chevin Road then left onto a footpath by 'Do not exceed 20' sign. In 150 yards turn right by metal gate. Over three stiles, straight ahead, hedge on right. Turn left on reaching hedge bordering golf course. Over small stream. Uphill diagonally across a field towards a stile in the wall ahead. Over the stile and turn left towards Hazelwood

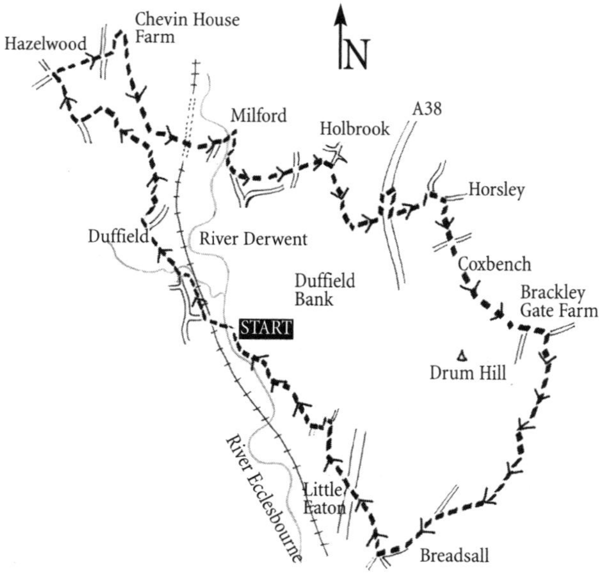

Hall Farm. Turn left up Spring Hollow and then right uphill at the junction towards St John's Church.

2 St John's Hazelwood to Holy Trinity Milford – 2.4 miles

Leave the church on Goodwin's Lane, approximately east. At the T-junction turn left, then at the end of a small car park turn right up a narrow track. Keep left and at the highest point straight on to eventually drop down to North Lane. Turn right and continue until Sunny Hill is reached, which drops away steeply to Milford. Cross the river bridge and turn left. Cross the road by the pedestrian crossing and turn left to Holy Trinity Church.

3 Holy Trinity Milford to St Michael's Holbrook – 1.4 miles

Leave the church and return towards the river bridge. Do not re-cross the bridge but carry straight on with the river on the right. Turn left up Holly Bush Lane and opposite the Holly Bush take the steps towards Holbrook. On reaching a road again, turn left and then right down Mellor's Lane. Turn right onto Church Street and St Michael's Church.

4 St Michael's Holbrook to All Saints' Breadsall – 5.5 miles

Leave the church downhill on Portway. Ignore footpath to Nether Farm. Take public footpath on left by 'Derestricted' road sign. Over small stream and railway line onto main Derby/Ripley road. Cross with care and turn left. Under A38 and take footpath off A38 Derby slip-road. Follow path round lower edge of very large field. After third stile turn left uphill, hedge on left. At top of hill, straight on, hedge on left. Follow path to right around boggy area and uphill to right of electricity pylon and church yard. Turn right on Church Street then right into French Lane. As the lane turns right, through a stile and take a path straight ahead which comes out onto Coxbench Road. Straight on onto Sandy Lane. In 1¼ miles, just after passing Quarry Road, turn right into The Croft. At the end of The Croft carry straight on through a stile by a gate and aim for a stile to the left of the farm buildings. Keep to left of farm buildings and straight on. Come out onto Brickkiln Lane. Straight across, onto a track behind houses. On reaching Morley Almshouses Lane, with multi-signed post, stay in field, straight on. Stay on track as it swings right and left and into the distance. After ¾ mile, by several large trees and two sets of new steel stiles on the left, turn right by a holly tree, keep hedge on right. Through break in hedge over field to come out onto Moor Road. Turn left to All Saints' Church. This is a fast and dangerous road. Take care.

5 All Saints' Breadsall to St Paul's Little Eaton – 1.3 miles

From the church take Rectory Lane, approximately north. Where the road bends right carry straight on through a gate and take a track which becomes a path. Immediately after passing under the A38 via a tunnel, turn right. Where the track turns left at the end of the waterworks, carry straight on over a small bridge. With a fence on the left keep to the right of farm buildings, over two small stiles and onto Alfreton Road. Turn right and continue, then cross the road by the pedestrian crossing at the school. Go down the road with the butcher's on the corner, over the railway line, turn left then right to St Paul's Church.

6 St Paul's Little Eaton to St Alkmund's Duffield – 1.5 miles

Leave the church on Vicarage Lane, approximately north. As the road bends to the right, take a path straight on. After the very narrow stile the path forks. Go left, down the bank. Turn left on stone track. Come out onto Eaton Bank and turn right. Turn left down a narrow path by electric gates towards the large chimney and follow the path with the river on the left back to the Bridge pub. Cross the river and back to the car park.

Walk 10

BELPER EAST AND WEST

Walk data

Distance:	7 miles
Height gain:	870ft
Toilets:	Belper, Strutt Street and the Triangle.
Refreshments:	Pubs and cafés in Belper; three pubs in Holbrook; Holly Bush pub, Makeney; pubs in Milford; Bluebell pub, Farnah Green.
Parking/Start:	Coppice car park, Belper. GR SK 351474

How to get to the start

On the A6 in Belper there is a junction for Morrisons supermarket. Turn up New Road, away from the supermarket. Through a set of pedestrian traffic lights, past a right turn and the Market Place is on the right. Enter the Market Place and the Coppice car park is to the right.

Route summary

Belper – Makeney – Farnah Green – Belper

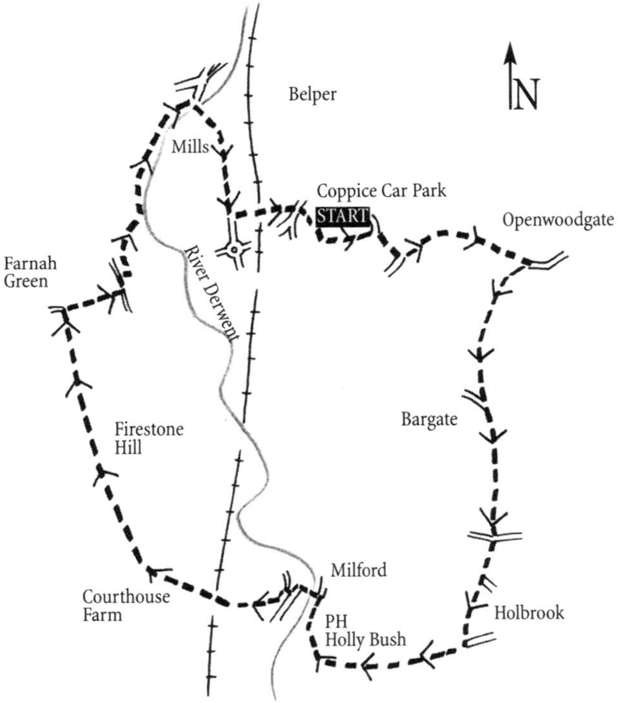

The route crosses the Coppice brook into the historic Belper Parks, part of the Royal Forest of Duffield Frith. Splendid panoramic views of both the east and west of Belper are seen.

ROUTE DETAILS

1 Coppice car park Belper to Holly Bush PH, Makeney – 3 miles

Leave the car park by steps on the eastern side, down to the brook and follow the path north-east. On reaching Mill Lane turn right and walk uphill. Turn left at the Kirk's Lane sign and follow the track uphill until Sandbed Lane is reached. Turn right up the hill. Carry on, past the White Hart PH, towards Holbrook. Pass the garage onto Makeney Road. Pass the very large house on the left. 10 yards after the sign to Holbrook & Coxbench (Mellor's Lane) turn right onto a path signposted 'Milford, 1'. Follow the path downhill to the Holly Bush. Just before the houses keep to the right of the holly tree and hedge. Down steps onto road.

2 Holly Bush PH, Makeney to end of North Lane, Farnah Green – 2 miles

Turn right and right again onto Makeney Road, past the garden centre, to the river bridge. Go over the bridge and turn right onto Chevin Road, via Chevin

Alley, then immediately left up Sunny Hill. It does eventually flatten out to become North Lane, a sandy track just over a mile in length. At the end of North Lane, before it bears sharp left towards Farnah Green Road, turn right on the path downhill.

3 North Lane, Farnah Green to Coppice car park, Belper – 2 miles

On reaching Chevin Road, turn left and, after 100 yards, turn right by the first farmhouse and drop down to the river. Follow the path roughly north back to Bridge Foot, go over the river bridge and walk along Bridge Street, turn left up King Street and back to the Coppice.

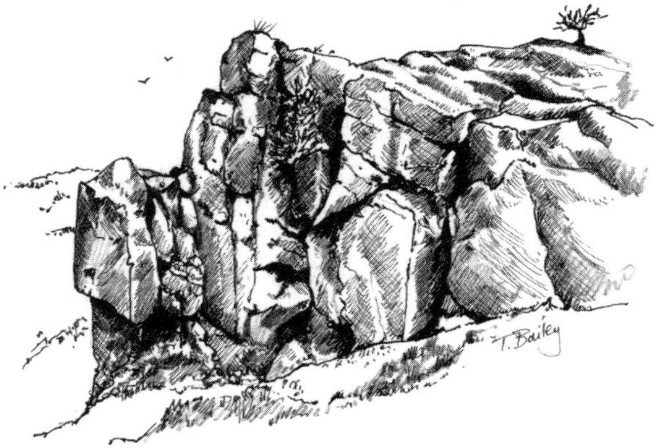

Walk 11

BELPER NORTH

Walk data

Distance:	16 miles
Height gain:	2,334ft
Toilets:	Strutt Street and the Triangle, Belper, Malt Shovel pub, Black Rock.
Refreshments:	Cafés and pubs in Belper. Malt Shovel pub overlooking Wirksworth.
Parking/Start:	Field Lane pay and display car park off Bridge Street, Belper. The start is the Triangle, Belper. GR SK 346479

How to get to the start

Leave the car park by the entrance used by cars, turn left and in a few yards turn right towards the large red-brick mill. The Triangle is by the traffic lights, before the mill is reached, once the terminus for buses.

Route summary

Belper – Coneygrave Hillock – Black Rock – Alderwasley – Belper

The route reaches some very high points within central Derbyshire, with views to match. The price to

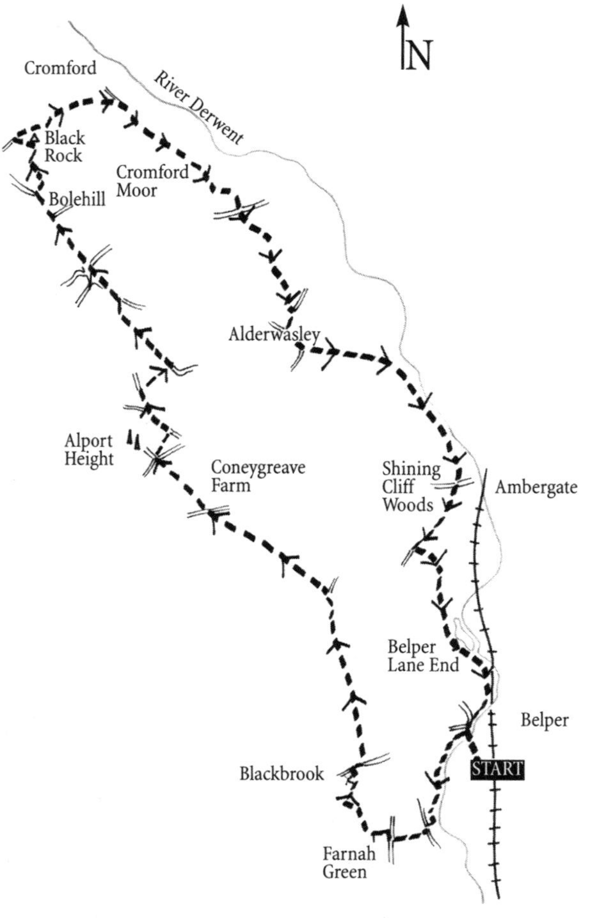
N
Cromford
River Derwent
Black
Rock
Cromford
Moor
Bolehill
Alderwasley
Alport
Height
Coneygreave
Farm
Shining
Cliff
Woods
Ambergate
Belper
Lane End
Belper
START
Blackbrook
Farnah
Green

pay is the long slog to Coneygrave Hillock. Also, after turning off Farnah Green Road, the route is on the lip of the Depths of Lumb. Until recently the Duffield Skyline route included a scramble up the side of this mini gorge, but we had to find a way around because the bridge had collapsed.

ROUTE DETAILS

1 Belper Triangle to Coneygrave Hillock – 4.7 miles

Leave Belper Triangle on Ashbourne Road, cross river on bridge by weir, immediately turn left onto waymarked lane which shortly becomes a field path. After two fields cross brook and drive, follow waymark, keep wall on your right. At the second gate in hedge go through a waymarked stile, follow path through wall and gap in hedge. Follow stone paved path to top of bank and aim for left-hand corner of wall skirting property. Over wooden stile into driveway to come out onto Chevin Road. Turn left and in 150 yards turn right onto signed footpath. Follow steep path with wall on your right for two fields and through stile onto ancient North Lane. Turn right and track shortly comes out onto Farnah Green Road. Turn right and in 100 yards turn left down a drive past a bungalow. Straight on over two wooden stiles towards stone steps. Over steps and follow path through a wood overlooking the Depths of Lumb. Into a field and follow a well-defined path onto Lumb Lane. Turn right. On reaching the A517 road at Blackbrook turn right, pass Plains Lane then turn left up Longwalls Lane. After 1½ miles turn left onto Wilderbrook Lane for 100 yards then turn right onto a path signed Midshires Way. After 1 mile the Midshires Way turns right, but carry straight on to Palerow Lane (Coneygrave Hillock).

2 Coneygrave Hillock to Black Rock – 3.8 miles

Leave Coneygrave Hillock by footpath opposite the one by which you entered the lane. Cross field to opening on left, onto track and go through gateway on your left. Aim for Alport pylons. Through stile to right of black water container, through two more stiles and, keeping wall on right, aim for stile in wall ahead between two trees. Onto Peat Lane and turn right. Path is to left of two trees and then to left of cypress hedge. Keep between wall and hedge, over stile by gates. Into Roughpiece Lane and turn left. On reaching road junction take right lane, Bent Lane. Take second signed path to right, by a gate inset from the lane, go to right of dead tree. Follow path over stiles and stream onto track. Across track leading to Colebrook Farm, follow waymark into wood. Onto road and turn left. Continue ahead on road for about a mile to pass the Malt Shovel and continue on Oakerthorpe Road for another ¾ mile. 200 yards after the road begins to descend turn right on waymarked path, up steps by first house in Bolehill. Follow well-marked path through field and wood to trig point (1,046ft). Continue on path and follow fence and blue posts down to the Black Rock picnic area (upper car park by toilets).

3 Black Rock to Alderwasley Church – 3.2 miles

From Black Rock to Alderwasley Park, follow the Midshires Way by leaving the picnic area eastward on the High Peak Trail. Pass the winding house and about 450 yards past the gate leave the trail by a path on the right, signed Alderwasley, keep to left of wooden fence and in a few yards there is another sign for Alderwasley. Follow the track, which turns right in about 300 yards and comes into a lane. Turn left and continue for about a mile, passing caravan sites and coming into a road where the footpath is immediately opposite. Go diagonally across field and through wood, coming out to left of farm buildings to join metalled road for 200 yards. Pass barn on right and take well-marked path on right. Straight on by gate with orange chain. Cross field and woodland path to lane, cross lane into paddock and then diagonally across field to corner by wood. Continue with wood on right and on crest of hill there is a gate and stile with a multiplicity of waymarks on the right. Go over stile and immediately turn left following Midshires waymark. Follow footpath across three fields. Stile in second field is by gate in top-right corner. Stile in third field is in top-left corner. Onto farm track to come out on road opposite Home Farm. Turn right up road and at junction continue straight on Higg Lane, signposted Alderwasley Church.

4 Alderwasley Church to Belper Triangle – 4.4 miles

Just past the church entrance there is a stile by a gate – our last Midshires Waymark. Go up track and just past memorial go left to a gateway by corner of playing field (plain waymark). Follow path on level to kissing gate in wire fence, continue through group of trees (noting 'neolithic' seat on right) to stile in wood. From this unmarked stile go straight on down main path, which in places is more like a stream. Ignore the path joining from the left and continue on steadily descending track. Shortly there is a chain-link fence on the left, then a metalled road. Continue on the road through factory. On leaving the factory area continue past another building and climb to join a metalled road. In a few yards there is a garage on the right and a woodland path forks to the right. Take this path to the right, which rises gently to come out onto Holly Lane. Cross the lane and continue on Whitewells Lane, signposted Blackbrook. In about ¾ mile there is a wood on the left. Immediately past the wood there is a stone stile on the left opposite a farm entrance. Go over the stile, down steps and follow the wall on the left to the next stile. Across a field to the bottom of wood on the right, follow wall on right to gate/stile. Continue straight ahead on farm track to gate/stile then turn right onto lane past target area of old firing range. Continue on lane which becomes Wyver Lane and come out into Bridge Foot. Turn left to cross the river to the Triangle.

Walk 12

ALLESTREE WEST

Walk data

Distance:	10 miles
Height gain:	730ft
Toilets:	Mundy Play Centre and Markeaton Park (slight diversion).
Refreshments:	Café in Markeaton Village and café in Markeaton Park.
Parking/Start:	Car park (free) on Woodlands Lane between Allestree and Quarndon, near the water tower. GR SK 341404

How to get to the start

The Quarndon end of Woodlands Lane is on Burley Lane. The Allestree end of Woodlands Lane is at the junction of Blenheim Drive, Allestree Lane and Birchover Way. The car park is between Allestree and the water tower.

Route summary

Allestree – Meynell Langley – Mackworth – Markeaton – Allestree

A gentle route apart from a limited exposure to the

Meynell
Langley
Upper
Vicarwood
N
Mackworth
Quarndon
Markeaton
Allestree
Water
Tower
START

A52. Approaching Upper Vicarwood, look towards Derby and view the effects of modern architecture. Notice the old pillbox at Meynell Langley with its view towards Derby and the façade of the Gatehouse to Mackworth Hall, a hall that was never built.

ROUTE DETAILS

1 Allestree to Meynell Langley Gardens – 3.7 miles

Leave the car park onto the road, turn right and in a few yards turn left following the sign 'Public Footpath'. Through a gate and straight on towards Kedleston Hall. At gap in hedge, straight ahead, hedge on right. On reaching facing hedge, turn right through gap in right-hand hedge. Over stile, stone wall on left. Over stile into Church Road. Turn left then in a few yards by a white square building turn right onto a path and up steps, over a lawn, over a stile then diagonally left towards a tree on the horizon. On reaching gatepost with waymark, diagonally right to stile. Over stile, take left option, hedge on left. Over stile, cross wooden bridge, over stile and follow waymark. Through metal gate onto track and road towards Kedleston Hotel and

Kedleston Road. On reaching Kedleston Road, turn left towards Derby and in 200 yards turn right onto path by metal gate and large tree. Hedge on right. Through gap in hedge then turn right. Keep hedge on right and progress to facing hedge in next field. Turn left and progress to bridge over brook. Over bridge and straight ahead across field. Through gap in hedge and straight ahead towards trees on horizon. Straight on through gap in hedge into woodland. Emerge from woodland, across field towards Mickleover water tower. On reaching tarmac track turn right until Upper Vicarwood Farm is reached. Continue through a gate on the left of the stable block and follow a grassy hilltop track. On reaching Lodge Lane, turn left towards Meynell Langley Gardens.

2 Meynell Langley Gardens to Mackworth Church – 2.4 miles

On reaching the gardens of Meynell Langley, turn left into a field before the drive, through a new wooden gate by an old pillbox. At gap in trees, by a metal gate, keep straight on. With trees on right, over stile by oak tree, over stile and down field, over stile into field. Aim for large tree central in broken-down hedge. Straight ahead to cross the wooden footbridge over brook. Up field to post with waymarkers by new gate and large tree. Follow marker indicating left. Through metal gate towards large trees, fence and Bowbridge Fields Farm on right. Through metal gate into large field, follow hedge on left. Walk to right of overgrown area and through stile onto A52 and turn left. Pass a garage and restaurant, then turn left along Jarveys Lane, through Mackworth Village. Where the lane turns sharp right, turn left and take the path passing in front of the church.

3 Mackworth Church to Allestree – 3.5 miles

Follow the Bonnie Prince Charlie waymarked route across fields to Markeaton. On reaching the road, take the path on the other side. Pass the garden centre and follow the road round to the left, over the bridge – note no footpath – then turn left just past the entrance to the Mundy Play Centre onto a track identified as 'Markeaton Stones'. Pass the new houses and farm and continue on a track. Eventually a surfaced lane is reached. Turn right. On reaching Kedleston Road, turn right then at the T-junction turn left towards Quarndon. After 200 yards turn right into Old Vicarage Lane following the signpost 'Public footpath to Allestree'. Keep to right of entrance pillars to number 12 towards stile, with hedges on left and right. Over stile, follow curved path, over small stream and turn left. Over stile, straight on uphill, over stile by holly trees and metal gate. On reaching brow of hill and gap in hedge, turn right onto original track back to car park.

Walk 13

CARSINGTON WATER – 1

Walk data

Distance:	5 miles
Height gain:	925ft
Toilets:	Pubs below.
Refreshments:	Pub in Carsington, two pubs in Brassington.
Parking/Start:	Sheepwash car park, Carsington Water. GR SK 249528

How to get to the start

Carsington Water is north-east of Ashbourne off the B5035 and south-west of Wirksworth on the road from the market place called West End which joins onto the B5035. The Sheepwash car park entrance is opposite the western entrance to Carsington and Hopton villages.

Route Summary

Sheepwash car park – Brassington – High Peak Trail – Sheepwash car park

Outstanding high-level views are to be seen of Brassington village and Carsington Water.

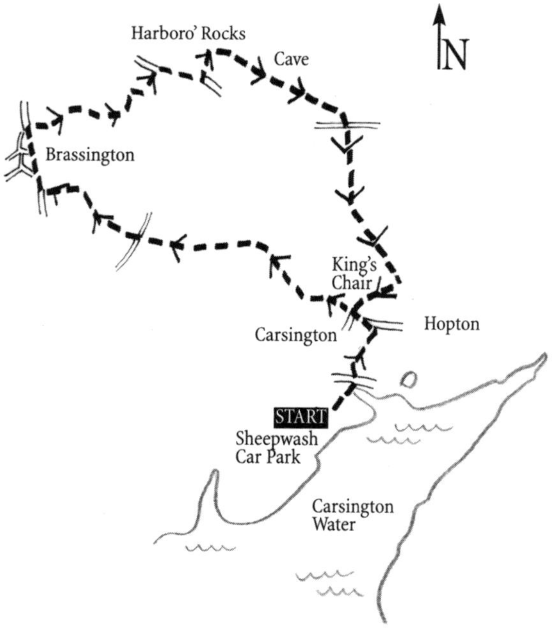

ROUTE DETAILS

1 Sheepwash car park to Brassington – 2 miles

Facing away from Carsington Water, set off on a path by the red 'No Entry' signs at the right-hand edge of the parking circle. It winds through trees to a main road, which you cross. Walk up a path, continue straight on when you meet a lane, then, on reaching the pub, turn left into Carsington village. Join the main road for a few yards then continue straight on, up a lane signed 'No Turning Space'. It becomes a track, rising steadily to a stile by a rusty five-barred gate. Continue on the track. Over a stile by two metal gates and a disused cattle grid. The path immediately bears right up a grassy bank to a V-shaped brow. Over a broken-down wall and keeping trees on your left, walk down fields to cross an old walled track. Follow the obvious path which soon divides; follow the sign just left of some old stone banking. Descend on a path, through stiles, into Brassington.

2 Brassington to the High Peak Trail – 1.2 miles

Turn right, up the road past Brassington Village Hall then right again at the village edge, up a lane. At the top turn left through a stile by a gate and follow the path by the fence, soon a wall, to the road. Turn right along the road then first left beyond the works entrance. The track leads to the High Peak Trail. Turn right.

3 High Peak Trail to Sheepwash car park – 2 miles

Along the trail, just before the next crossing, turn right through a stile signposted 'Carsington'. Cross the road and follow the wall on the left, which eventually comes up against a wood. Turn right and follow the fence-line down a steep bank to a gate by a cottage. The end wall of the cottage has a window and a black drainpipe. Descend the steps and the slope into Carsington. Turn left. Retrace the route back to Sheepwash car park.

Walk 14

CARSINGTON WATER – 2

Walk data

Distance:	14 miles
Height gain:	1,868ft
Toilets:	As below.
Refreshments:	Carsington Visitor Centre; pub in Carsington; two pubs in Brassington.
Parking/Start:	Carsington Visitor Centre car park – pay and display. GR SK 241516

How to get to the start

Carsington Water is north-east of Ashbourne off the B5035 and south-west of Wirksworth on the road from the market place called West End which joins onto the B5035. The Visitor Centre is off the road that connects the B5035 near Knockerdown with Hulland Ward.

Route summary

Visitor Centre – Brassington – Hopton Crossing – Hopton Turning – Visitor Centre

Outstanding high-level views are to be seen of Brassington village and Carsington Water. The High

Peak Trail follows the original Cromford and High Peak Railway route from High Peak Junction to Whaley Bridge, a distance of 33 miles, and was opened fully in 1831. In spring the wild flowers are abundant.

ROUTE DETAILS

1 Visitor Centre to Brassington – 3.4 miles

Leave Visitor Centre going north, following the yellow waymarked walkers signs to Sheepwash. On reaching Sheepwash, set off on a path by the red 'No Entry' signs at the right-hand edge of the parking circle. It winds through trees to a main road, which you cross. Walk up a path, continue straight on when you meet a lane, then, on reaching the pub, turn left into Carsington village. Join the main road for a few yards then continue straight on, up a lane signed 'No Turning Space'. It becomes a track, rising steadily to a stile by a rusty five-barred gate. Continue on the track. Over a stile by two metal gates and a disused cattle grid. The path immediately bears right up a grassy bank to a V-shaped brow. Over a broken-down wall and keeping trees on your left, walk down fields to cross an old walled track. Follow the obvious path which soon divides; follow the sign just left of some old stone banking. Descend on a path, through stiles, into Brassington. Cross the road and walk up the hill to the Miners Arms.

2 Brassington to Hopton Crossing – 3.3 miles

Continue up hill to church, enter churchyard at corner and keeping church on right, walk to far wall. Turn right following new footpath sign up steep bank onto lane. Turn left in lane for 100 yards and take stile on right opposite a chapel. Climb obliquely left between outcrop sand on a clear path. Rainster Rocks come into view on the left. Go through stiles to farm buildings. Pass the farm on the right, keep farmyard wall on your left to gate into lane. Turn right up lane to join a road shortly. There go right again (beware traffic on sharp bend) and in 400 yards go under a bridge and then right to get onto the High Peak Trail. On getting on the trail turn left (south-east). Walk on the trail for about two miles. There is a gate across the trail and an access road to works crosses it.

3 Hopton Crossing to Hopton Turning – 2.5 miles

Continue on the trail for just over a mile down Hopton incline, through a tunnel, and where there is a gate across the trail, go through it and bear right. Turn right before a building and down steps to a stile. Turn right, keeping the wall on your right and head for a ladder stile at the end of the next field, then left to a gate onto lane. Turn right up lane for about 100 yards then left through a waymarked stile. Keep parallel with wall on your left for three fields. At the stile in the third field Carsington Water is visible again. Continue across field to stile to left of rocks, path continues to right of miners' old spoil heaps to come into a green lane. Turn left on the lane and then cross the lane and over stile into field and aim for the ladder stile in wall to right of wood. Go diagonally across next field to bottom-right corner by wood and onto road.

4 Hopton Turning to Visitor Centre – 2.5 miles

Cross bypass road with care and turn right towards Ashbourne. Walk on the grass verge. In about 100 yards take waymarked path on the left. You are now back on the Carsington circular way. After 300 yards on the path, turn left at yellow waymarked sign over stile into field. Over metal gate up path across field to waymarked stile. Follow sign keeping to right of a clump of trees on top of hill to come out on lane. Turn right up lane and follow signpost to Kirk Ireton. Just past the top of the rise there is a crossroads. Turn right down Blind Lane. On reaching junction of Blind Lane, Benthead Lane and Old Field Lane, continue on Benthead Lane. Benthead Lane becomes Broom Lane. On reaching Hays Lane, take the footpath parallel to Hays Lane, eventually reaching a track heading for the water. Just before this track turns sharp right, turn left and follow the yellow walkers' signs back to Millfields picnic area. Continue over the dam wall back to the Visitor Centre.

Walk 15

CHATSWORTH – 1

(CLOCKWISE ROUTE)

Walk data

Distance:	6 miles
Height gain:	1,100ft
Toilets:	Garden Centre, Chatsworth House, Edensor village shop/café, which asks for a small charge for non-customers.
Refreshments:	Garden Centre; Chatsworth House; Edensor village shop/café.
Parking/Start:	Calton Lees car park on the Chatsworth estate. GR SK 259684. This is a pay car park with a manned kiosk.

How to get to the start

The Calton Lees car park is adjacent to the Garden Centre in Chatsworth Park on the B6012 between Rowsley and Baslow.

Route Summary

Calton Lees car park – Chatsworth House – Calton Lees car park

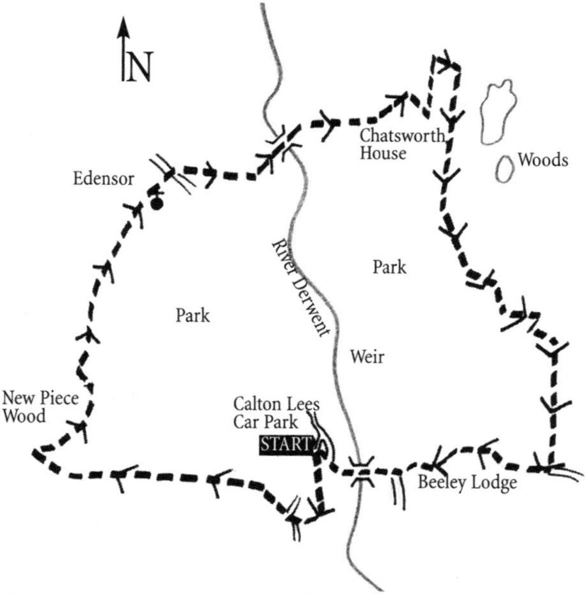

This route combines a walk in the park with a steep climb up 144 steps and a stroll through woods, with some views to be remembered.

ROUTE DETAILS

1 Calton Lees car park to Chatsworth House – 2.9 miles

From the southern end of the car park take the road by

the sign 'No Through Road'. In about 300 yards, at a grass triangle in Calton Lees, keep straight on through the middle gateway of three, signed 'Please keep dogs on leads'. Follow the track for about a mile. The end of it winds right and then left through a gate to pass Calton Houses. 100 yards beyond the last cottage go through a gate and turn right. Follow the wall on your right for about 200 yards then bear left away from the wall across the field. Pass a barn on your right and Russian Cottage, away on the right. Through gate and follow the wide woodland track through New Piece Wood. Through another gate. Bear slightly right downhill to a waymarked post. Pass a fenced copse on your right then go downhill to pass another fenced copse on your right. At the fence corner straight on to a waymarked post. Walk down the field keeping the spire of Edensor Church to your right. Pass another waymarked post. Climb four steps to go through a small iron gate. Follow the path and steps into Edensor village. Turn right. Follow the village road down to and through the gate. Cross the B6012 Park Road and follow the gravel path, which bears right over a small hill to reach the bridge over the River Derwent at Chatsworth House. Cross the bridge then turn right to follow a path that leads, via a small gate, up to the clock tower archway.

2 Chatsworth House to Calton Lees car park – 1.8 miles

At the archway turn left following signs to 'The Farmyard'. At the driveway turn right to a gate and cattle grid by the 'Adventure Playground' sign. A few yards further on bear second right following the 'Stand Wood Walk' route. In about 100 yards, beyond a sharp right-hand bend, turn left opposite a rough layby and barn, just before a low stone marked with coloured arrows. Follow a narrow woodland track uphill. Straight across a track following purple and blue arrows and a stream before climbing the 144 steps to the Hunting Tower. On reaching the driveway turn left for a few yards then turn right following purple arrow up a short flight of steps. Pass in front of the tower until a sunken door in the tower at the bottom of steps is visible. With your back to the door walk forward to enter the wood on a narrow hidden path, following purple arrow. Follow the path through the wood for nearly ½ mile. Take care, it is a slippery path with steep drops on right. Climb the short flight of steps near the waterfall. Continue up six more steps to a wide track and turn right. Follow the track for ½ mile to a surfaced drive and turn left.

At a crossroads of tracks turn right following the 'Hob Hurst's House, Beeley' sign. Cross a stile by a gate into open moorland. Follow a wide track for about 150 yards. Turn right at a waymarked sign 'Concessionary Path'. Follow the rocky path downhill through bracken. Go over a new stile and cross the field to Beeley Hilltop. Aim for the farm buildings. Cross the stile or go through the gate and turn right down the lane. In ½ mile turn right along the B6012 to cross the bridge back into the park. In a few yards, by the house, turn left then turn right up a path signed 'Footpath to Rowsley'. This takes you to the Chatsworth Garden Centre and back to the car park.

Walk 16

CHATSWORTH – 2

(ANTI-CLOCKWISE ROUTE)

Walk data

Distance:	6 miles
Height gain:	1,100ft
Toilets:	Garden Centre; Chatsworth House; Edensor village shop/café, which asks for a small charge for non-customers.
Refreshments:	Garden Centre; Chatsworth House; Edensor village shop/café.
Parking/Start:	Calton Lees car park on the Chatsworth estate. GR SK 259684. This is a pay car park with a manned kiosk.

How to get to the start

The Calton Lees car park is adjacent to the Garden Centre in Chatsworth Park on the B6012 between Rowsley and Baslow.

Route summary

Calton Lees car park – Chatsworth House – Calton Lees car park

This route combines a stroll through woods with a steep descent down 144 steps and a walk in the park, with some views to be remembered.

ROUTE DETAILS

1 Calton Lees car park to Chatsworth House – 1.8 miles

Leave car park towards Garden Centre. On road down to Garden Centre turn left into wood. On leaving wood turn left on track towards road. On reaching road turn right and over river bridge. In 200 yards turn left uphill signposted 'No Through Road'. In ½ mile just past farmyards turn left over stone stile into field. Across field to obvious stile. Over stile and turn left on path uphill through bracken. On reaching top, turn left on track towards wood. Over stone step stile into wood. In 200 yards, where tracks cross, turn left, signposted 'House'. After 250 yards, where metalled track continues ahead and downhill, take rough track to right. After ¾ mile, where tracks cross, turn left down stone steps to pool, overlooking the House. Turn right down steps. Continue to right on path. Beware steep and dangerous drop on left. Arrive at Hunting Tower. Continue along front of tower, down steps onto road and turn left. In 10 yards turn right onto path downhill. Down 144 stone steps. Take extreme care. Continue downhill, over stream. On reaching crossroads of tracks continue straight across. On reaching road by small stone hut turn right, downhill to the House.

2 Chatsworth House to Calton Lees car park – 2.9 miles

Round front of restaurant block and turn right downhill towards car park kiosk. Past House entrance downhill towards river bridge. Over bridge and take wide track to right towards Edensor. Cross road. Through right-hand gate into Edensor village. Straight ahead, keep to right of church. 200 yards past church turn left up steps, signposted 'Footpath to Rowsley, 3 miles'. Through metal gate, progress to skyline. Keep to right of large central wood. Keep to right of next wood and aim for wooden gate to the left of three seats. Enter track into wood over stone step stile or through gateway. Exit wood and continue straight ahead across field. Keep straight ahead at signposts downhill towards right-hand telephone line post. Continue downhill with wall on your left. Turn left through wooden gate into wood. Down track to left. On track through Calton Houses. Down long track and on reaching a crossroads of tracks continue straight on, back to Calton Lees car park.

Walk 17

HOLLINS CROSS AND MAM TOR

Walk data

Distance:	4½ miles
Height gain:	1,126ft
Toilets:	Castleton car park and opposite Speedwell Cavern on the Winnats Pass.
Refreshments:	Castleton – cafés and pubs.
Parking/Start:	Castleton car park – pay and display. GR SK 149829

How to get to the start

The car park is adjacent to the Information Centre on the western side of the village on the A625.

Route summary

Castleton – Hollins Cross – Windy Knoll – Castleton

The quality of the views makes up for the short distance and the pain on the steep slope, with views of the face of Mam Tor, up to Hollins Cross. From here there is the panorama of the vale of Edale. But it is not over, there is the drag to the top of Mam Tor. Then down the Winnats Pass. Is it worth it? It certainly is. Walking does not get any better than this!

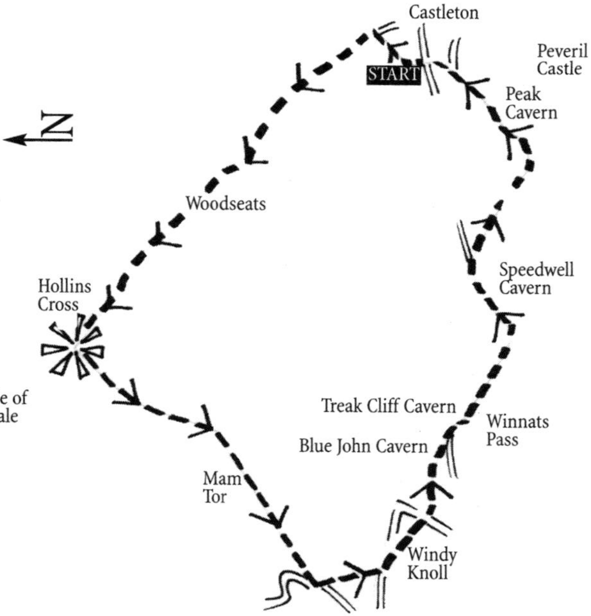

ROUTE DETAILS

1 Castleton car park to Hollins Cross – 1.4 miles

Leave the car park at the bottom-right corner. Emerge onto Millbridge and turn left. Cross a bridge over a stream, keep on road past cemetery. Follow road to left at Hollowford Centre. At next T-junction follow road to left. Where road bends to left, carry straight on over stile/through gate up wet track signposted 'Public Bridleway, Hollins Cross'. Through gate into open country, follow track up hill to left. Over stile onto steep paved track to Hollins Cross.

2 Hollins Cross to Windy Knoll – 1.2 miles

Turn left onto paved track, through two gates to the top of Mam Tor. This is a dangerous area. Keep to the path. Continue down paved path onto road.

Turn left down paved steps, through gate signposted 'Windy Knoll'.

3 Windy Knoll to Castleton car park – 1.8 miles

Through gate onto road, cross road and through gate opposite. Follow stone track and after a few yards turn left onto grass track, farmhouse straight ahead. Through gate, cross road, through another gate into field. Follow yellow arrow on gatepost. Through gateway, follow wall on right. At end of farm wall walk towards gateway and onto Winnats Pass. Follow road downhill. Just past Speedwell Cavern turn right through gate into Longcliffe. Through gate with wall on left. Follow track downhill with wall on left towards wood. Through gate at corner of wood, down path and road, over stream. Turn left to follow path by side of stream and return to car park.

Walk 18

OGSTON RESERVOIR

Walk data

Distance:	6 miles
Height gain:	760ft
Toilets:	None
Refreshments:	None
Parking/Start:	Car park by Ogston Sailing Club. GR SK 374604

How to get to the start

The car park is off Quarry Lane, which is off the B6014 between Tansley and Stretton, which is near Clay Cross.

Route summary

Ogston Reservoir – Highoredish View Point – Ogston Reservoir

Mainly fields and numerous stiles, with some road walking. No significant climbs. Good views from Highoredish View Point.

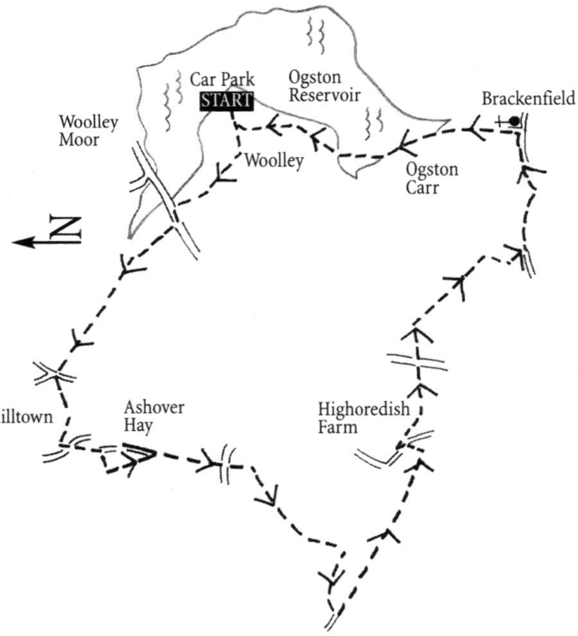

ROUTE DETAILS

1 Ogston Reservoir car park to Highoredish View Point – 3.1 miles

Leave the car park, walk back to the B6014 Stretton/Tansley road. Cross the road and take the signed footpath to the left of Smithy Cottage. Through a gateway to a stile. Over next stile by large bush into wood.

Continue over three more stiles and onto muddy track. On reaching the road turn left and in 20 yards turn right through stone stile. Straight across field, over stone stile, through gateway, wall on left, go around boggy area to stile at top left-hand corner of field. Turn right by entrance to Hay View and walk down to road. Turn left by sign 'The Hay'. Walk on road and after 200 yards turn right by 'No Through Road' sign, also signed 'Greenfields Farm'. Turn left into Greenfields Farm, through stile by gate, next stile is a set of steps set into a wall by a gate. Keep wall on right, over similar stile, across field towards track. Over wooden stile, through metal gate onto road. Turn right on road. On reaching T-junction on B6014 carry on straight across down track. Through gateway, stream on left. Over ford. Trees on right through stone stile. Keep trees on right, through stile by large tree. Turn left, keep wall on left up large field to stone stile in top left-hand corner. Through this stile and immediately turn right through stone stile to left of stone building. Up cobbled and concreted road and after 100 yards turn right by yellow arrows on tree onto green track. Follow the track up the hill, which eventually opens out into a field, with views of the reservoir. Keep to left of derelict barn and through wooden stile onto road. Turn left on road. Halfway down wood on right, turn left into Highoredish View Point.

2 Highoredish View Point to Ogston Reservoir car park – 2.5 miles

Leave Highoredish View Point and turn left onto the road. Turn left at Highoredish Farm (a bungalow) and down a steep bank onto a minor road. Turn left. In 100 yards there is the entrance to a farm with a signpost – 'Holiday Cottages' and 'Highoredish Farm'. Follow the right-hand sign for 'Highoredish Farm' towards Fairytail Shetland Pony Stud. Over stile into field. Head for left-hand side of wood. Over wooden stile into wood, down path. Through stone stiles down field, wall on left. Over stone stile onto road. Turn left and after 50 yards turn right over wooden stile by metal gate into field. Keep hedge on left. At end of field by metal gate, do not leave field but turn right, keep ditch on left. Over wooden stile and wooden footbridge. Keep ditch and hedge on left. Over wooden stile, hedge on left. Over wooden stile by metal gate onto track. Walk on track to road. Leave Carr Lane, turn left down hill, past Teapot Farm to church. Follow road round to left and walk on road back to the car park.

Walk 19

TISSINGTON – 1

Walk data

Distance:	6 miles
Height gain:	840ft
Toilets:	Tissington car park.
Refreshments:	Cafés in Tissington; butcher's in Tissington; Bluebell Inn pub on the A515 near the southern entrance to Tissington.
Parking/Start:	Tissington car park, pay and display. GR SK 177521

How to get to the start

There are two entrances to Tissington from the A515 between Newhaven and Ashbourne and one entrance from the B5056 between Fenny Bentley and Longcliffe. Cars may be parked opposite Tissington Hall, but the main car park is past the duckpond, keep right and the car park is on the right, actually on the Tissington Trail.

Route summary

Tissington car park – Alsop en le Dale Station – Tissington car park

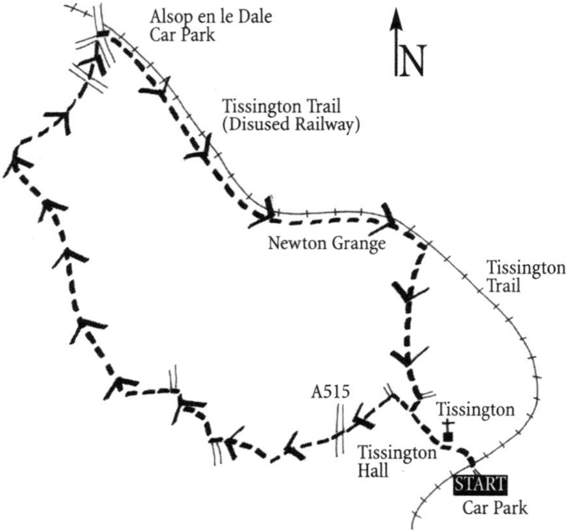

Tissington Hall was built in 1609 and is the home of the FitzHerbert family. The church dates back to Norman times. On Ascension Day six wells are dressed with religious themes as thanksgiving for the water supplies from the wells. A wooden frame is filled with clay and mosses and flower petals are pressed into the clay to make a colourful display.

ROUTE DETAILS

1 Tissington Car Park to Alsop en le Dale Station – 3.3 miles

Leave car park, walk back to the road, turn left back to the village then right to pass Tissington Hall. At the road junction carry straight on and in 100 yards turn left onto a path signed 'Public Footpath'. The next stile is to the right of a small red-brick building. Continue across a field to the road, the A515. Cross with extreme care. Down to bottom of field to wooden gate. Across field, next stile is a ladder stile by left small tree. Straight up field towards large tree. Over ladder stile. Diagonally right uphill between two trees, continue to top and over stone steps to left of metal gate and onto road. Turn right. After 350 yards turn left by large metal gate over stile and continue uphill. Just before an old brick kiln, turn right through a stile. Continue through a gateway and over two stiles into a farmyard. Keep to the right of the farm buildings, exiting by the farm track. As the track sweeps to the right take the path straight ahead. Over ladder stile and downhill towards gate. Through stile to next waymark post which indicates a left turn, keeping wall on right. Stile is to left of gate in facing wall at top of field. Follow track with Alstonefield Church ahead. At the track to Hanson Grange take the path to Alsop en le Dale. Follow track downhill past New Hanson Grange to a lane. Go straight across this lane, over the field, then cross A515 road with extreme care and enter Alsop en le dale Tissington trail car park.

2 Alsop en le Dale Station to Tissington – 2.9 miles

Leave the car park towards the south. After the first bridge ignore a sign to the right 'Public Footpath, Tissington'. Proceed along the trail. Immediately after the next bridge there is a sign on the left 'Public Footpath – Follow wall to bridge'. Take this path. Turn left over bridge, through farmyard and over stile uphill towards stile by post. Follow waymarks and posts through fields towards Tissington. On reaching the road, turn right then left past Tissington Hall and back to the car park.

Walk 20

TISSINGTON – 2

Walk data

Distance:	10 miles
Height gain:	1,720ft
Toilets:	Tissington car park; Milldale; Alstonefield.
Refreshments:	Cafés in Tissington; butcher's in Tissington; Bluebell Inn pub on the A515 near the southern entrance to Tissington; café in Milldale; the George pub in Alstonefield.
Parking/Start:	Tissington car park, pay and display, GR SK 177521

How to get to the start

There are two entrances to Tissington from the A515 between Newhaven and Ashbourne and one entrance from the B5056 between Fenny Bentley and Longcliffe. Cars may be parked opposite Tissington Hall, but the main car park is past the duckpond, keep right and the car park is on the right, actually on the Tissington Trail.

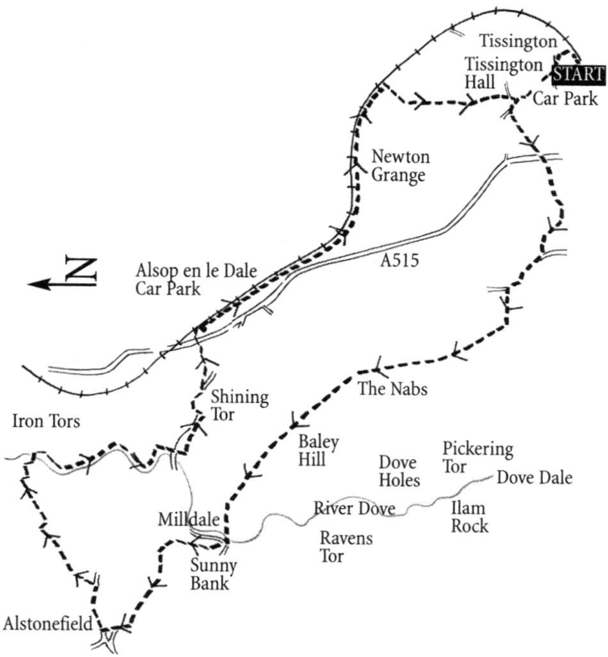

Route summary

Tissington – Milldale – Alstonefield – Alsop en le Dale Station – Tissington

Tissington Hall was built in 1609 and is the home of the FitzHerbert family. The church dates back to

Norman times. On Ascension Day six wells are dressed with religious themes as thanksgiving for the water supplies from the wells. A wooden frame is filled with clay and mosses and flower petals are pressed into the clay to make a colourful display. At Milldale is Viator Bridge. Viator means traveller, and the bridge is named after a character in Izaak Walton's book, *The Compleat Angler*, which first appeared in 1653.

ROUTE DETAILS

1 Tissington Car Park to Milldale – 3.6 miles

Leave car park, walk back to the road, turn left back to the village then right to pass Tissington Hall. At the road junction carry straight on and in 100 yards turn left onto a path signed 'Public Footpath'. The next stile is to the right of a small red-brick building. Continue across a field to the road, the A515. Cross with extreme care. Down to bottom of field to wooden gate. Across field, next stile is a ladder stile by left small tree. Straight up field towards large tree. Over ladder stile. Diagonally right uphill between two trees, continue to top and over stone steps to left of metal gate and onto road. Turn right. After 350 yards turn left by large metal gate over stile and continue uphill. Just before an old brick kiln, turn right through a stile. Continue through a gateway and over two stiles into a farmyard. Keep to the right of the farm buildings, exiting by the farm track. As the track sweeps to the right take the path straight ahead. Over ladder stile and downhill towards gate. Through stile to next waymark post which indicates a left turn, keeping wall on right. Stile is to left of gate in facing wall at top of field. Follow track with Alstonefield Church ahead. At the track to Hanson Grange take the path to Milldale. Straight on through a stile by two metal gates. Straight on by two more metal gates, downhill through gates and stile, then down a very steep zigzag path to Milldale.

2 Milldale to Alstonefield – 0.9 miles

Pass by front of shop, pass the public phonebox. Continue on lane uphill, past church on left and follow lane/road into Alstonefield and the village centre by the George.

3 Alstonefield to Alsop en le Dale station – 2.6 miles

Follow the road signposted 'Lode Mill 1, Ashbourne 7'. After a short distance, ignore the first public footpath sign 'Narrow Dale/Gypsy Bank', but take the next track signed 'Youth Hostel' and 'Coldeaton Bridge via Gypsy Bank'. Continue down track and path, eventually arriving at the top of Gypsy Bank. Descend the steep hill with care. Cross the river bridge and turn right. Follow the track by the side of the river until the road is reached. Turn left up the hill but take the alternative route avoiding the road up Shining Tor. On reaching a signpost 'Tissington, 2½ miles' return to the road, uphill. Take the road to the left signed 'Parking 440 yards'. Cross the A515 road with extreme care and enter Alsop en le Dale station Tissington Trail car park.

4 Alsop en le Dale station to Tissington – 2.7 miles

Leave the car park towards the south. After the first bridge ignore a sign to the right 'Public Footpath, Tissington'. Proceed along the trail. Immediately after the next bridge there is a sign on the left 'Public Footpath – Follow wall to bridge'. Take this path. Turn left over bridge, through farmyard and over stile uphill towards stile by post. Follow waymarks and posts through fields towards Tissington. On reaching the road, turn right then left past Tissington Hall and back to the car park.